GW01607679

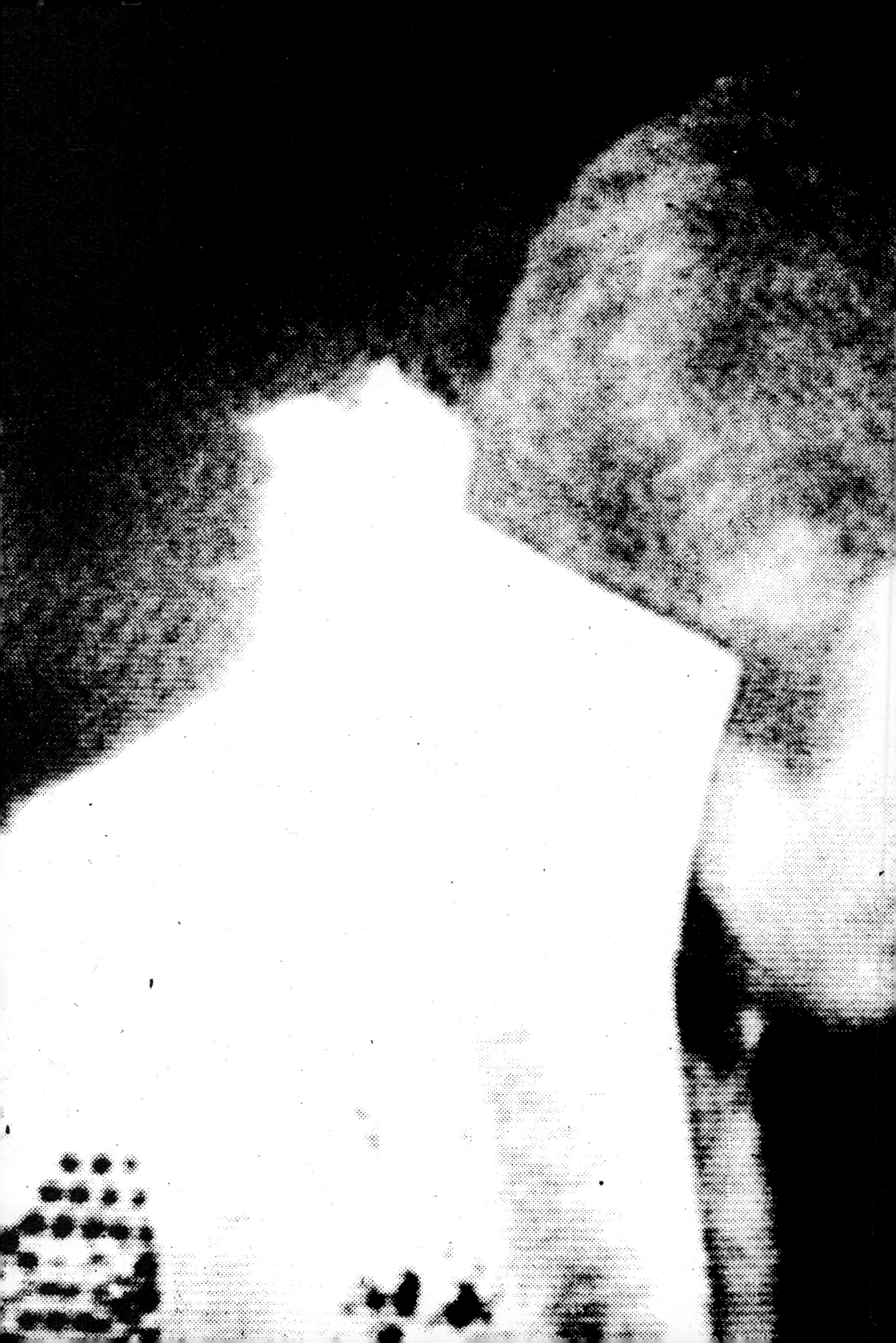

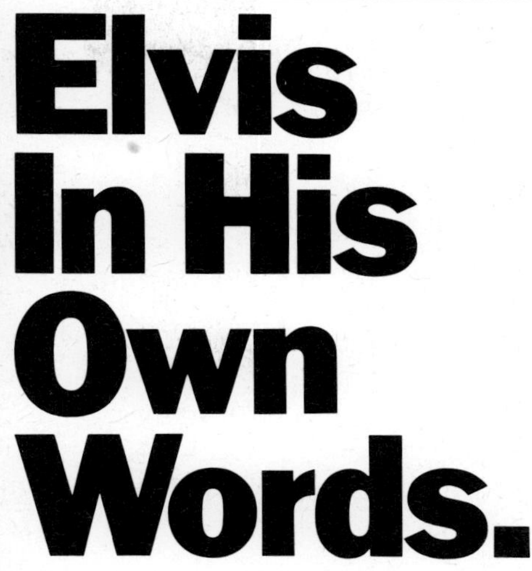

Compiled by Mick Farren.
Designed and edited by
Pearce Marchbank.

W H Allen, London.
A Howard & Wyndham Company.
1981.

Introduction.
Page 7

The Early Messages To Fans.
Page 9

Elvis On Rock'n'Roll.
Page 25

Elvis Remembers His Childhood.
Page 29

The Early Legend.
Page 35

The Movies.
Page 45

Elvis On Girls.
Page 53

Elvis Faces The Fifties Press (Part One).
Page 59

Elvis And Uncle Sam.
Page 73

Elvis And Colonel Tom.
Page 79

Elvis And Recording.
Page 83

Elvis And The Critics.
Page 89

Elvis On Graceland.
Page 97

Elvis Faces The Fifties Press (Part Two)
Page 101

The Last Statement To The Press.
Page 119

The material in this book comes from a number of sources.
They include:
"The Truth About Me" (a widely circulated fan record) recorded 1956,
"Elvis" by Jerry Hopkins,
Interview with Lionel Crane, *Daily Mirror,* 1955,
New Musical Express 1956,
"Elvis Sails" RCA EP 1958,
"TV Guide Presents Elvis" 1958,
Interview with Hy Gardner WABD TV New York, 1956,
Radio interview, Wichita Falls, Texas, 1956,
Dick Clarke interview 1959,
Press conference, Vancouver, 1957,
"The Radio Luxembourg Book of Record Stars" 1962,

ISBN 0 491 02776 1

Printed in England by
South Western Printers Ltd., London and Caerphilly.,
for the Publishers W H Allen & Co. Limited,
London W1X 8LB

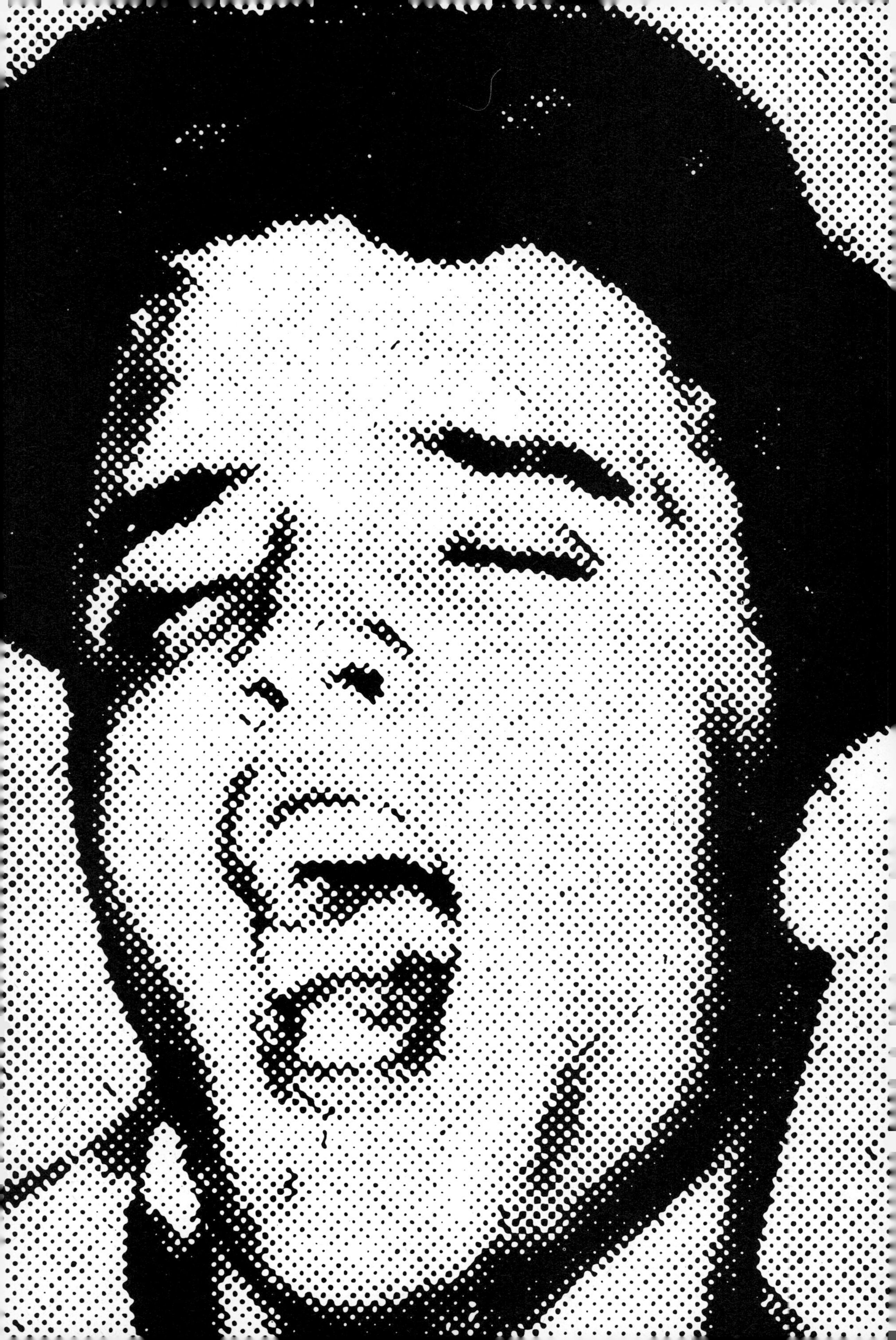

Probably one of the greatest tragedies that surround the life of Elvis Presley is the way we will never know what the man thought or felt. For a superstar who was an object of affection for literally millions of fans, Elvis Presley's personality was virtually a closed book.

Elvis Presley rose to fame before the media had started treating musicians as potentially serious, thinking people with ideas worth listening to and opinions worth hearing. Nobody bothered with long, searching interviews back in those days. It would be another ten years before any rock and roller would grace the pages of *Playboy* with an in depth interview.

Not that Presley was unwilling to talk, back in the fifties. In fact it was quite the reverse. On the way up, Elvis seemed perfectly willing to talk to anyone. Unfortunately, the probing questions were never asked. Nobody seemed interested in what Elvis Presley thought about the cold war, Eisenhower or even music. Mostly the questions in those early days stuck to the well tried, patronising path that the fifties press tended to adopt towards any new phenomenon. What was his favourite colour? How many cars did he have? What did he eat for breakfast? What kind of girls did he like?

After Elvis came back from his stint in the US Army, however, the interviews stopped. He no longer bothered to make even the blandest or most banal statement. For ten years there was silence.

It was only at the very end of the sixties that we were allowed the slightest glimpse of the Presley character. In his 1969 TV spectacular, when he returned to rock and roll, suited out in black leather and looking lean and tough, he let a few pearls fall in the asides between songs. He laughed and joked and even let the world know that he liked the Beatles and the Byrds.

During the early seventies Elvis Presley became a great deal more public. He played regular live concerts and even gave a major press conference in New York.

Sadly, that was the last chance the media had to confront Elvis Presley. He would never sit down with a Jann Wenner or Dick Cavett and bare his soul to the millions of curious fans.

All we have left are fragments: whatever is still preserved from the comparatively few press conferences and radio interviews. Even these limited remnants, when carefully edited together, do start to create a picture of Elvis Presley, particularly the young Elvis Presley, as he recounts his rise from truck driver to superstar.

It may not be a complete picture, but it's more than we've had before ... let Elvis tell it in his own words. *Mick Farren.*

The Early Messages To Fans.

Hi, this is Elvis Presley. I guess the first thing people want to know is why I can't stand still when I'm singing. Some people tap their feet, some people snap their fingers, and some people just sway back and forth. I just started doing them all together, I guess. Singing rhythm and blues really knocks it out. I watch my audiences and I listen to them and I know that we're all getting something out of our system but none of us knows what it is. The important thing is that we're getting rid of it and nobody's getting hurt.

I suppose you know I've got a lot of cars. People have written about it in the papers and a lot of them ask me why. Well, while I was driving a truck, every time a big shiny car drove by it started me sort of daydreaming. I always felt that some day, somehow, something would happen to change everything for me, and I'd daydream about how it would be.

The first car I ever bought was the most beautiful car I've ever seen. It was second-hand, but I parked it outside my hotel the day I got it and stayed up all night just looking at it. And the next day it caught fire and burned up on the road.

In a lot of the mail I get people ask questions about the kind of things I do and that sort of stuff. Well, I don't smoke and I don't drink and I like to go to the movies. Maybe some day I'm gonna have a home and a family of my own and I won't budge from it. I was an only child, but maybe my kids won't be. I suppose this kind of talk raises another question: Am I in love? No. I've thought I've been in love but I guess I wasn't. It just passed over. I guess I haven't met the girl yet, but I will, and I hope it won't be too long, because I get lonesome sometimes. I get lonesome right in the middle of a crowd. I get a feeling that with her, whoever she may be, I won't be lonesome any more.

Well, thanks for letting me talk to you and sort of get things off my chest. I want to thank all my loyal fans who watch my performances and who in a way have become friends of mine. I sure appreciate you listening to my RCA Victor records and I would like to thank the disc jockeys for playing them.

WITH FANS IN 1966

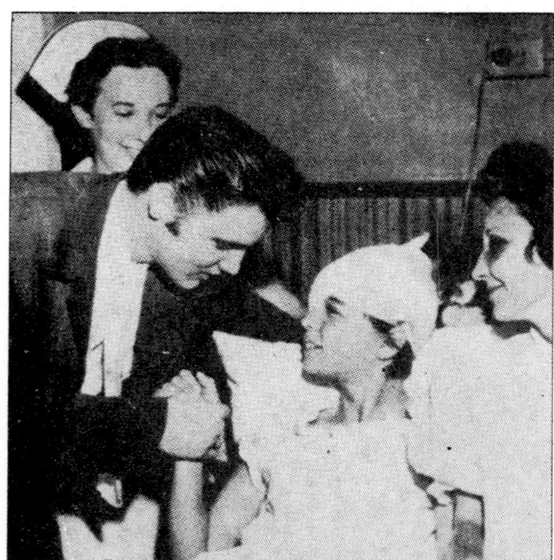
A 1957 HOSPITAL VISIT

I'm afraid to wake up each morning. I can't believe all this has happened to me. I just hope it lasts.

Thanks to all my faithful teenage fans, I have made a lot of money all of a sudden. Just two years ago I was driving a truck for $35 a week in Memphis, Tennessee, and before that I was knocking down $14 a week (that's less than £5 in your money) as a theatre usher.

Then one day my father gave me a guitar. Although I didn't know a B-flat from C-sharp, I finally learned to play.

My career as a singer started by accident. I went into a record shop to make a record for my mother, just to surprise her. Some man in there heard

AUTOGRAPHED LINCOLN, 1956

me sing and said he might call me some time. He did . . . a year and a half later.

He was Sam Phillips, the owner of Sun Records, and I made a couple of records for him. Mr. Steve Sholes, who is the head of country-western music at RCA Victor, happened to hear one of them and wanted to sign me up with his company.

It was Mr. Sholes who gave me "Heartbreak Hotel" to cut and, as you know, it turned out to be a million seller.

A lot of people ask me where I got my singing style. Well, I didn't copy my style from anybody. I've got nothing in common with Johnnie Ray, except that we both sing — if you want to call it

HYSTERIA, 1956

singing.

I jump around because it is the way I feel. In fact, I can't even sing with a beat at all if I stand still.

The kids are really wonderful the way they respond to my style. I get around 10,000 fan letters a week. So many people all over the country are starting fan clubs for me.

I certainly am grateful to them all, and in answer to some of the questions they ask, here are a few statistics about myself.

I was born in Tupelo, Mississippi, on January 8, 1935. I was raised and went to high school in Memphis, Tennessee, which is still my home. I never

In Person
ELVIS PRESLEY

took any singing lessons, and the only practising I ever did was on a broomstick before my Dad bought me my first guitar.

I'm six feet tall and weigh 195 pounds. I've gained about twenty pounds in the last year. I can't understand that because my appetite isn't as good as it used to be. I don't have much time for regular meals any more, because I'm always travelling around the country, working in a different city every day.

I usually gulp down a quick sandwich in between shows, but when I can, I enjoy having a big dinner with three pork chops and plenty of mashed

BREAKFAST TIME, 1957

potatoes and gravy.

I understand there have been a lot of rumours concerning me, I am beginning to think that they have more rumours about me than records. A while ago, they thought I was dead. Well, I'm as alive and kicking as I'll ever be.

I can't seem to relax ever, and I have a terrible time falling to sleep at night. At the most I usually get two or three hours of broken sleep. There was even a wild rumour that I shot my mother. Well, that is pretty silly. She's my best girl friend, and I bought her and Dad a home in Memphis, where I hope they'll be for a long, long time. I made

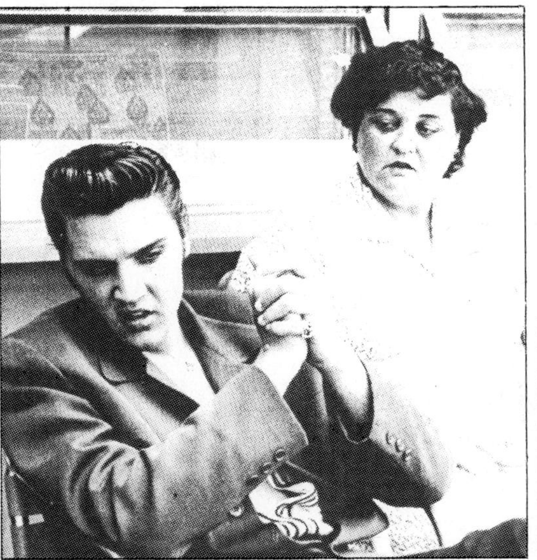

WITH HIS MOTHER IN 1957

my father retire a few months ago. There isn't much sense in his working, because I can make more in a day than he can make in a year. There were some rumours, too, about my getting married. Well, I have no plans for that, and I am not engaged. I guess I just haven't found the right girl yet. Besides records and personal appearances, I am looking forward to making a movie. I took a screen test a couple of months ago and Paramount Pictures signed me to a contract. I may make a picture before the end of the year.

In fact, everything is going so fine for me that I can't believe it's not a dream. I hope I never wake up.

ELVIS WITH FRIENDS

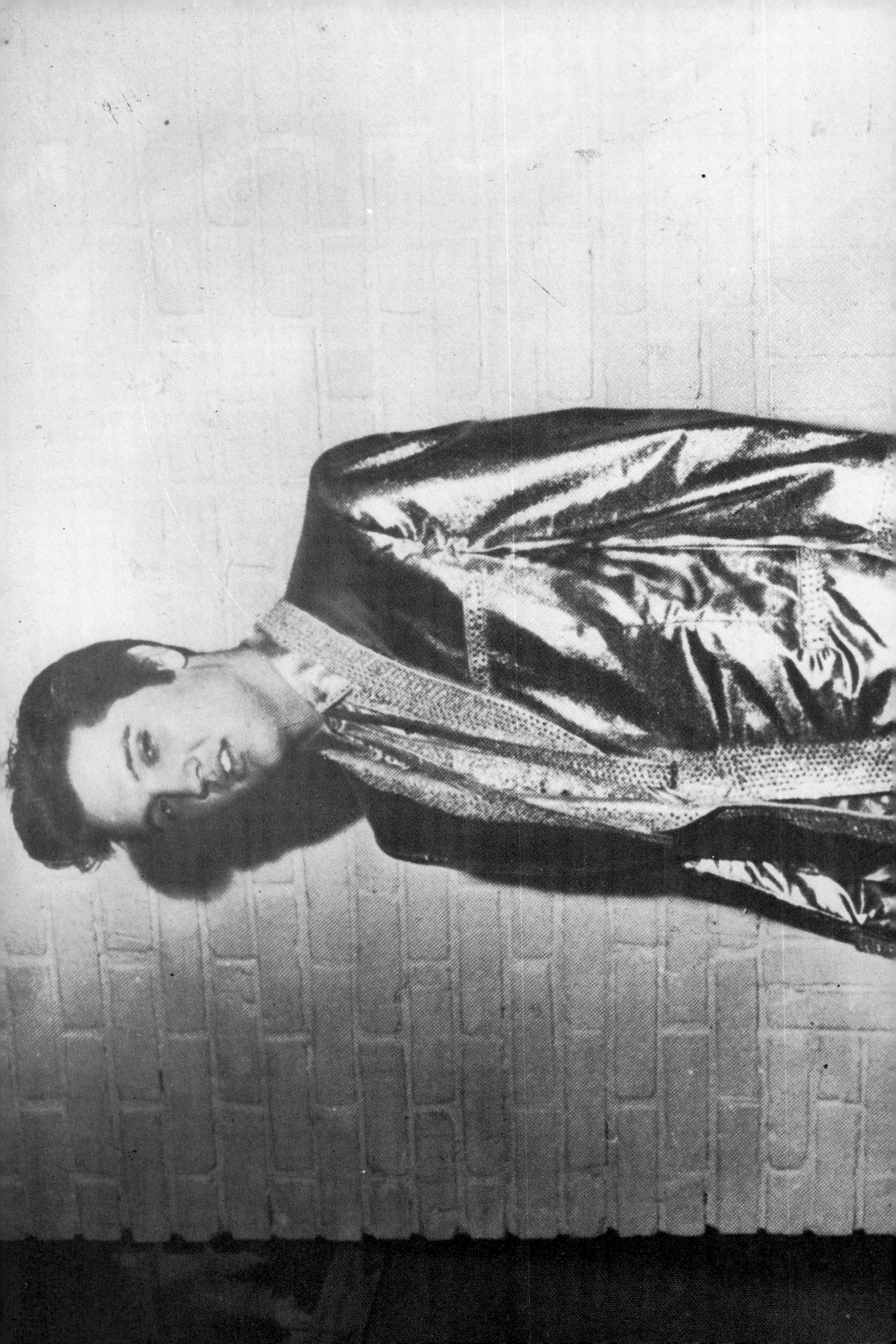

Elvis on Rock 'n' Roll.

Rock and roll has been around for many years. It used to be called rhythm and blues. And as far back as I can remember it's been very big, although in the last five years it's gotten much bigger. But personally I don't think it'll ever die completely out because they're gonna have to get something mighty good to take its place.

Rock and roll music, if you like it and if you feel it, you can't help but move to it. That's what happens to me, I can't help it.

I don't see that any type of music would have any bad influence on people. It's only music. I can't figure it out. In a lot of the papers they say rock and roll is a big influence on juvenile delinquency. I don't think that it is, juvenile delinquency is something, I don't know how to explain but I don't see how music has anything to do with it

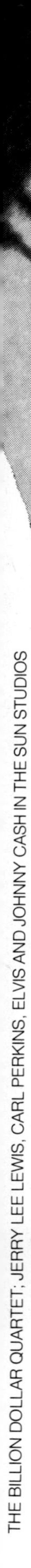

THE BILLION DOLLAR QUARTET; JERRY LEE LEWIS, CARL PERKINS, ELVIS AND JOHNNY CASH IN THE SUN STUDIOS

at all. I mean, how would rock and roll music make anybody rebel against their parents?

I've been blamed for just about everything wrong in this country. Juvenile delinquency, for example. that I give kids "ideas", whatever that means. I'm vulgar, they say. I wouldn't do anything vulgar in front of anybody, 'specially children. My folks didn't bring me up that way.

I don't do anything bad when I

work. I just move to the music 'count of it's the way I feel it. I hear it and I gotta move.

It's hard to explain rock 'n' roll. It's not what you call folk music. It's a beat that gets you. You feel it.

If I wasn't sincere, I'd just leaf through my work and say "Gimme my money and I'll get the hell out."

When I don't do a good job, I know it and I'm blue as hell. You'll pardon my language, but I mean it.

Elvis Remembers His Childhood.

ELVIS WITH HIS PARENTS, AGED TWO

My mama never let me out of her sight. I couldn't go down to the creek with the other kids.

Sometimes, when I was little, I used to run off. Mama would whip me, and I thought she didn't love me.

We were a religious family, going round together to sing at camp meetings and revivals. Since I was two years old, all I knew was gospel music. That music became such a part of my life it was as natural as dancing. A way to escape from the problems. And my way of release.

During the singing, the preachers would cut up all over the place, jumping on the piano, moving every which way.

The audience liked them. And I guess I learned a lot from them.

We were broke, man, broke, and we left Tupelo overnight.

Dad packed all our belongings in boxes, and put them on the top and in the trunk of a 1939 Plymouth.

My daddy was a common labourer. He didn't have any trade, just like I didn't have. He mostly drove trucks, and when he used to bring the truck home from the wholesale grocery, I used to sit in it by the hour.

I used to get mad at Mama once in a while. But I guess a growing boy always does. I was the only child and Mama was always right with me. Maybe she was too good.

I could wake her up in the middle of the night if I was worried about something. She'd get up, fix me a sandwich and a glass of milk, and talk to me; help me figure things out.

ELVIS AT THIRTEEN YEARS

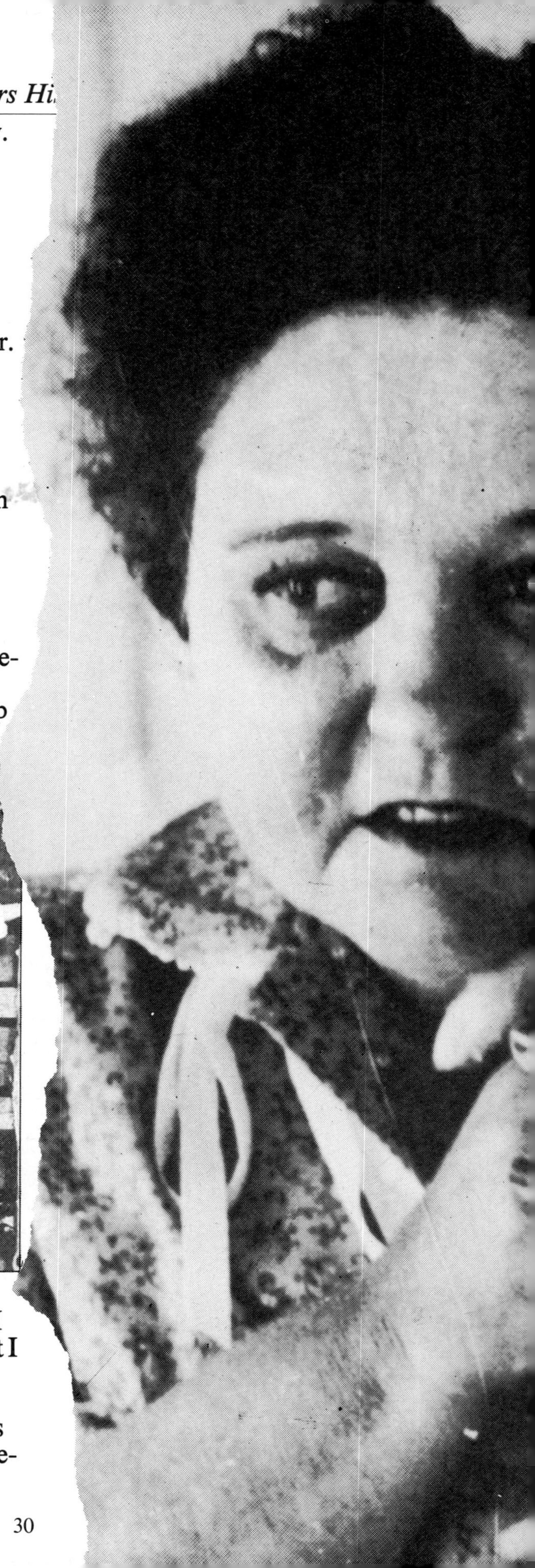

My mother, I suppose because I was an only child I was a little closer, I mean, everyone loves their mother but I was an only child and my mother was always with me, all my life, and it wasn't only like losing a mother, it was like losing a friend, a companion, someone to talk to. I could wake her up any hour of the night and if I was worried or troubled about something she'd get up and try to help me. I used to get very angry at her when I was growing up, it's a natural thing, isn't it? A young person wants to go somewhere, do something,

ELVIS WITH HIS FATHER'S CAR, AGED EIGHTEEN

and your mother won't let you and you think well, what's wrong with you? But later on in years you find out that she was right, that she was only doing it to protect you and keep you from getting into trouble and getting hurt. And I'm very happy that she was kind of strict.

ELVIS IN THE LOCAL CADET FORCE

MRS. GLADYS PRESLEY

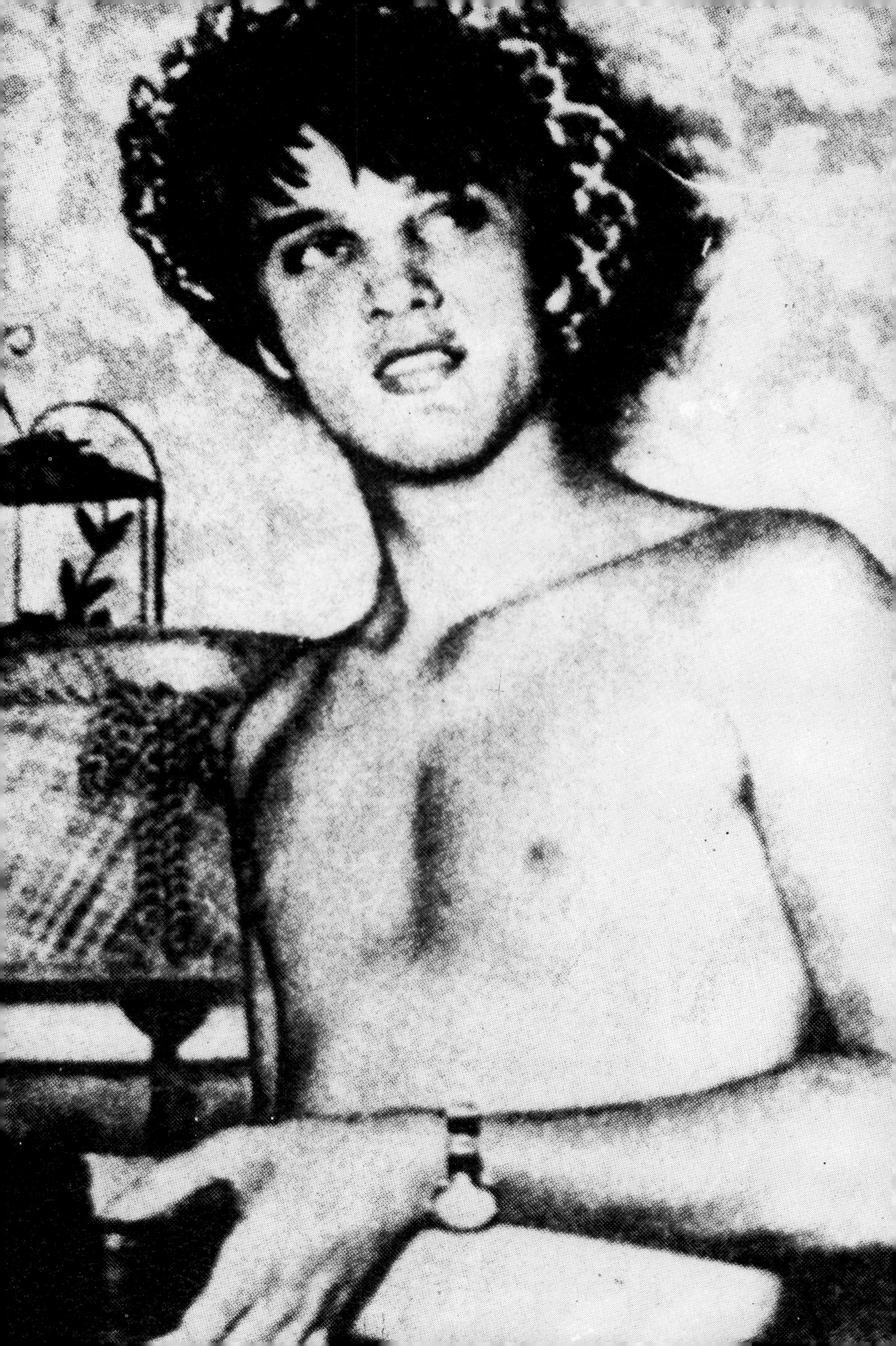

The Early Legend.

IN ACTION IN MEMPHIS, 1956

From the time I was a kid, I knew something was going to happen to me. I didn't know exactly what, but it was a feeling that the future looked kinda bright.

I wanted to be a singer, because I didn't want to sweat. I had a job driving a truck when I got out of high school. After that, I got a job at a dollar an hour in a defence plant. Then, when I first started singing, I figured it was for me.

My daddy knew a lot of guitar players, and most of them didn't work, so he said, "You should make your mind up to either be a guitar player or an electrician, but I never saw a guitar player that was worth a damn!"

I was driving a truck. That was back in Memphis, where I live. I was trying to say, I was learning to be an electrician. I was driving a truck and I was studying to be electrician, too, you see.

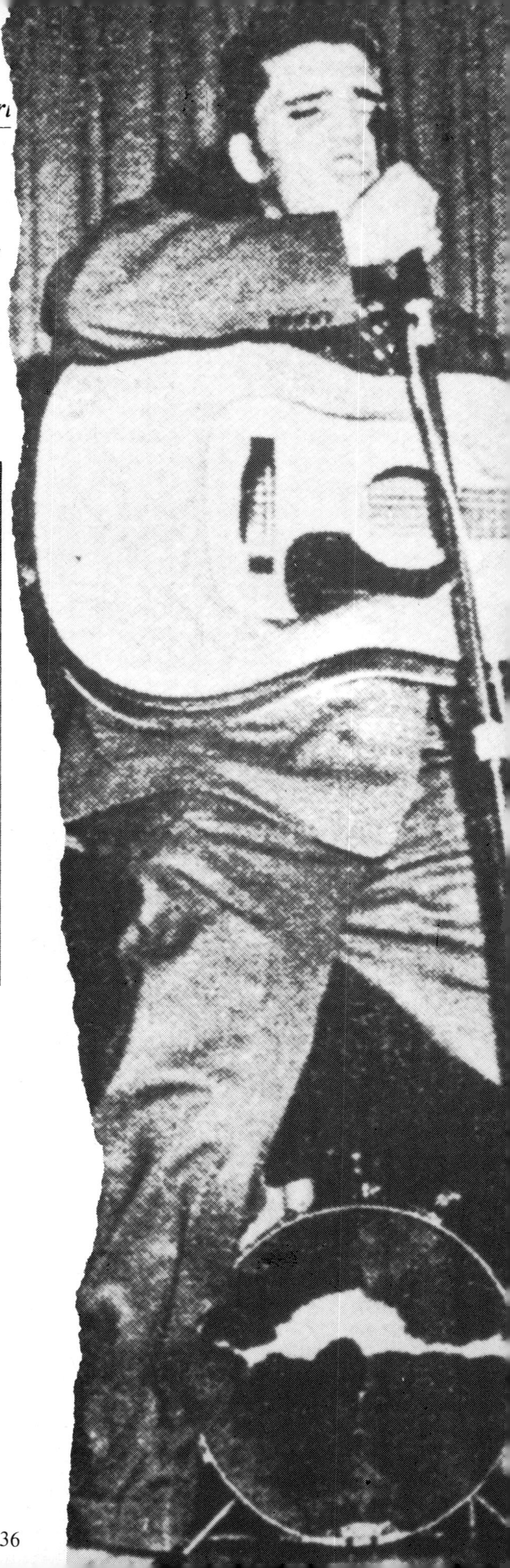

Well, I went into Sun Records and there was a guy there that took down my name and told me he might call me some time, so he called me about a year and a half later. I went in and I made my first record, "That's All Right".

"You want to make some blues?" he (Phillips) suggested over the phone, knowing I'd always been a sucker for

SAM PHILLIPS OF SUN RECORDS

that kind of jive. He mentioned Big Boy Crudup's name and maybe others, too. All I know is, I hung up and ran fifteen blocks to Mr. Phillips's office before he'd gotten off the line — or so he tells me. We talked about the Crudup numbers I knew — "Cool Disposition", "Rock Me Mama", "Hey Mama", "Everything's All Right" and others, but settled for "That's All Right". I wasn't known at all until Colonel Parker started managing me, you see, and then I got on RCA Victor and on television.

I was known in certain sections, you know, but I wasn't known all over.

The first time I sang in public was at an amateur programme at a fair. I

COLONEL TOM PARKER

wasn't doing this type of song that I do now. Nobody knew what rock and roll was back in those days. It's not like you hear it on the radio, when you do it on the stage, you have to put on a show for people. People can buy your records and hear you sing, and they don't have to come out to hear you sing. You have to put on a show to draw a crowd. If I just stood up there and sang and never moved, people would say, 'I could stay home and listen to his records.' You have to give them a show, something to talk about.

My very first appearance after I started recording, I was doing a show in Memphis where I started, a big show in an outdoor auditorium. I came to stage and I was scared stiff. It was my first big appearance in front of an audience. I came out and I was doing a fast type tune, one of my first records, and every-

FANS INVADE A MIAMI THEATRE IN 1956

body was hollering and I didn't know what they were hollering at. Then I came off stage and my manager told me that everyone was hollering because I was wiggling. So I did a little more and the more I did, the more I got.

I just fell into it, really. My daddy and I were laughing about it the other day. He looked at me and said, "What happened, El? the last thing I can remember is I was working in a can factory, and you were driving a truck." We all feel the same way about it still.

I went down there to the Louisiana Hayride just to try it out, more or less. I went down once and I went back again a couple of weeks later and the people, they seemed to kind of go for my songs a little bit so they gave me a job.

I've been very lucky. I've been very lucky. I happened to come along at a time in the music business when there was no trend. I was very lucky. The people were looking for something different and I was lucky, I came along just in time.

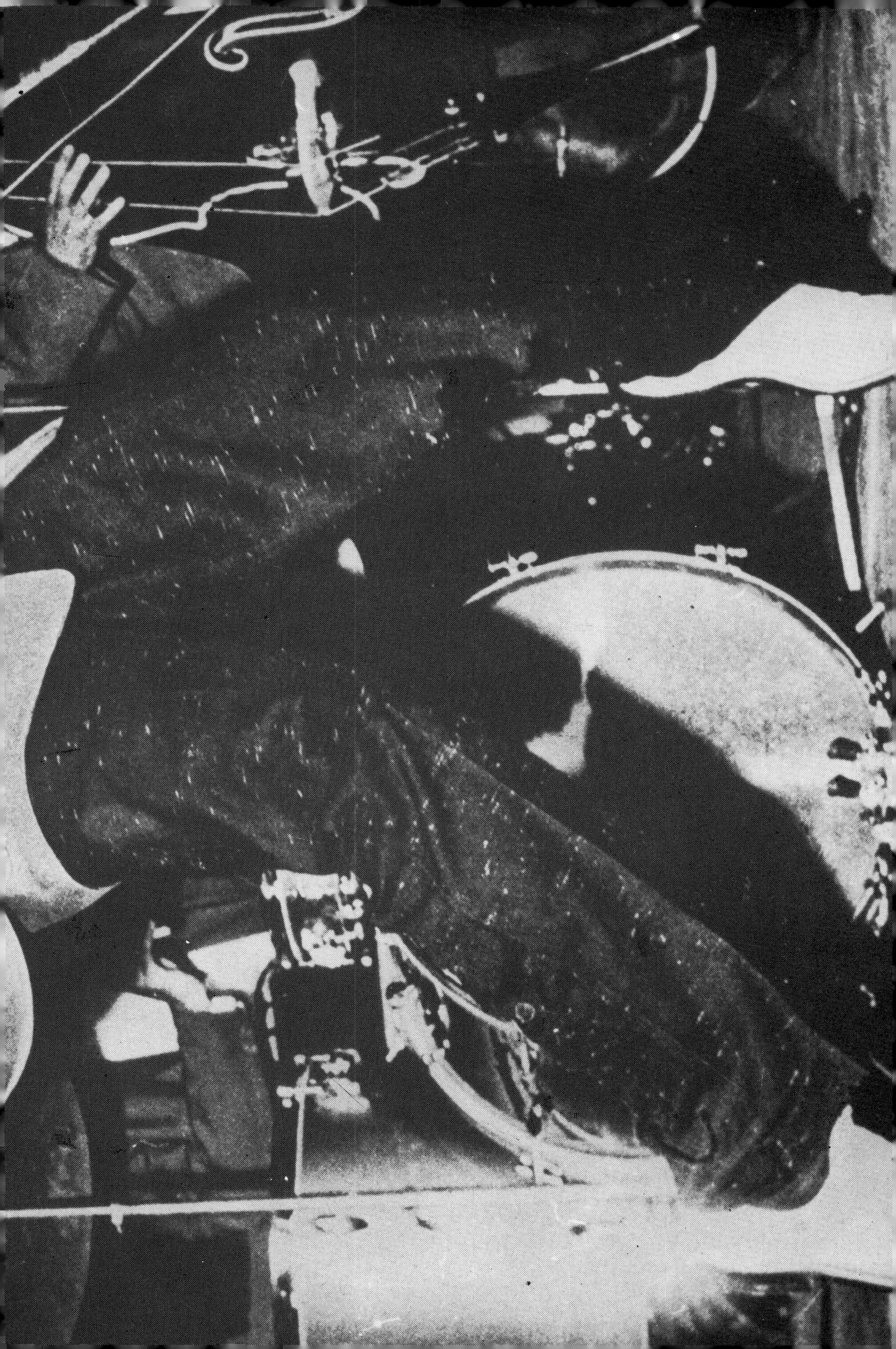

The Movies.

'PARADISE-HAWAIIAN STYLE', 1966

If I were a good actor, and of course I'm not a good singer, but if I were a good actor I think I would like it a little better, although if I ever break into acting completely I'll still continue singing, I'll still continue making records.

We got a seven year contract with Paramount Pictures. We have a movie coming out, I don't know when but we start making it in June. It's a movie with Burt Lancaster and Katherine Hepburn called "The Rain Maker".*

Am I a rock 'n' roller, and balladeer, or a movie actor? I feel I can do both and not let one interfere with the other. I stop thinking of my guitar when I step on a movie stage.

The effect I have on audiences mostly comes from simple rhythm.

* This 1956 statement refers to a movie debut project that was dropped in favour of "Love Me Tender".

Rhythm is something you either have or don't have, but when you have it, you have it all over.

I don't believe in Stanislavsky or whatever those methods of acting are called. I have never read Stanislavsky and don't intend to. I don't believe in drama teachers either. Why should I? The director I work with is my teacher for the time being and anything he tells me goes.

Why should there be another guy explaining to me what the director wants when I can ask him myself?

I go to the movies. I'm a movie fan. me and the boys take off at any time to take in a movie, and there isn't a week-end we don't take in two. We go to any movie house. I've seen some movies half a dozen times when it's got some-

'JAILHOUSE ROCK', 1957

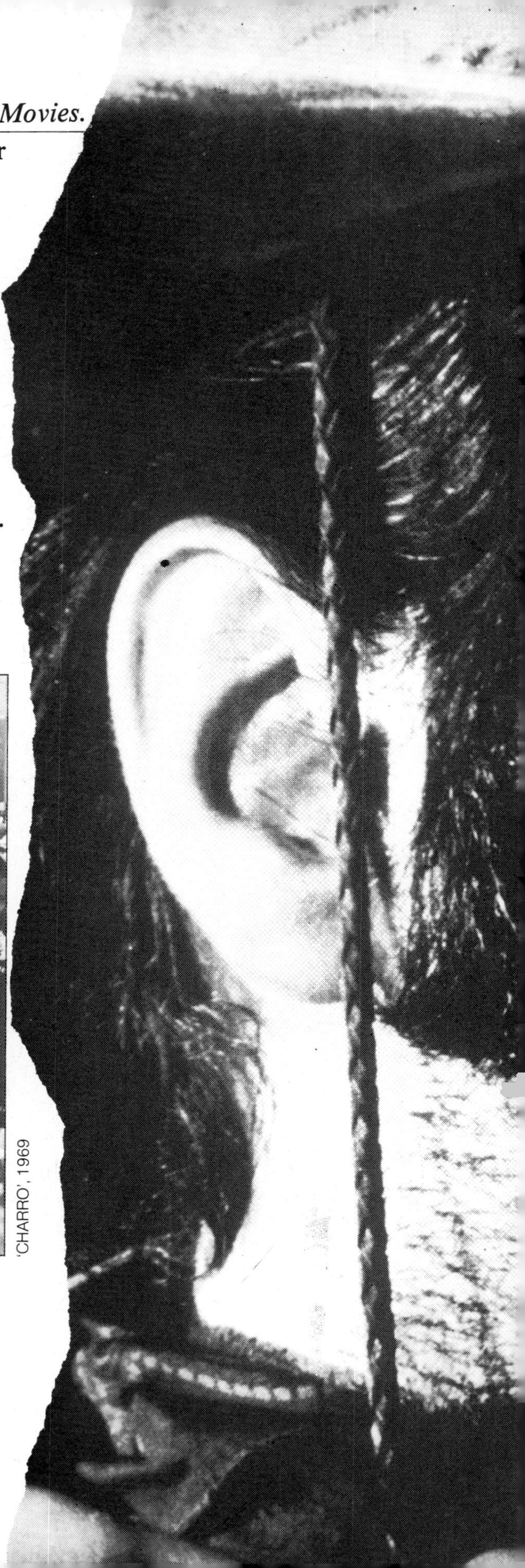

'CHARRO', 1969

thing to say by way of interesting acting.

I like movies better than I do TV because you've got more time to — if you goof, in a movie, you just go back and take it over. On TV you just goof.

Well, there's nobody that helps you out. They have a director for the

G·M

'LOVING YOU', 1957

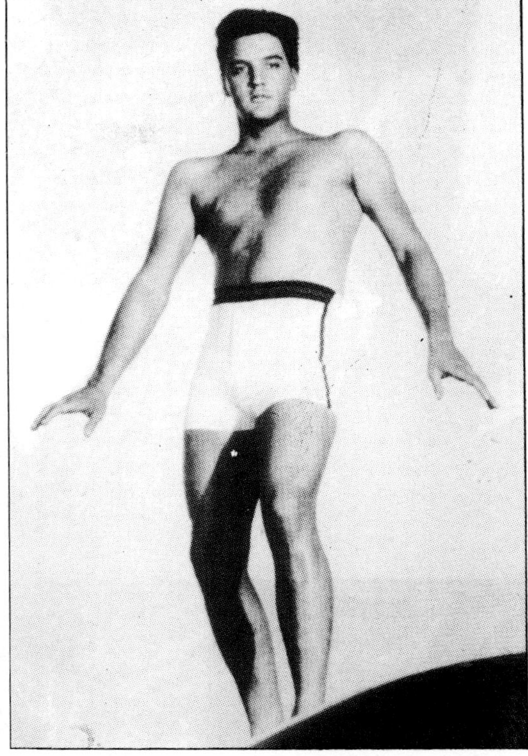

'BLUE HAWAII', 1961

'JAILHOUSE ROCK', 1957

'HARUM SCARUM', 1965

scenes, as far as the acting, and as far as singing and all, you're on your own. Nobody tells you how to do that, you have to learn it yourself.

I would never compare myself in any way to James Dean because James Dean was a genius. I sure would like to, I mean, I guess a lot of actors in Hollywood would like to have the ability that James Dean had, but I would never compare myself to James Dean in any way.

My favourite actors are Marlon Brando and Spencer Tracy.

How do you rate yourself as an actor?

Pretty bad. I mean, it's something you learn . . . and I think I might accomplish something at it, through the years.

Acting natural, don't you do that, in your last two pictures?

In some scenes I was pretty natural in others I was trying to act and when you start trying to act, you're dead.

Elvis on Girls.

I was makin' it with girls everywhere I went.

Those girl fans would throw their handkerchiefs at me and I'd blow my nose on 'em and toss 'em right back and them ladies would hug their hankies to their breasts and never wash 'em. That's devotion for yah.

Elvis, what's your idea of the ideal girl?

Female, sir . . . I really don't know. I like a lot of different types. I suppose I'll know if I ever find someone that I really fall in love with.

What do you think of young actresses as dates? How do they compare with the girls back home?

Well, they're just like everybody else. They just got lucky, the same as me.

ELVIS WITH STRIPPER TEMPEST STORM, YVONNE LIME & WITH BARBARA LONG

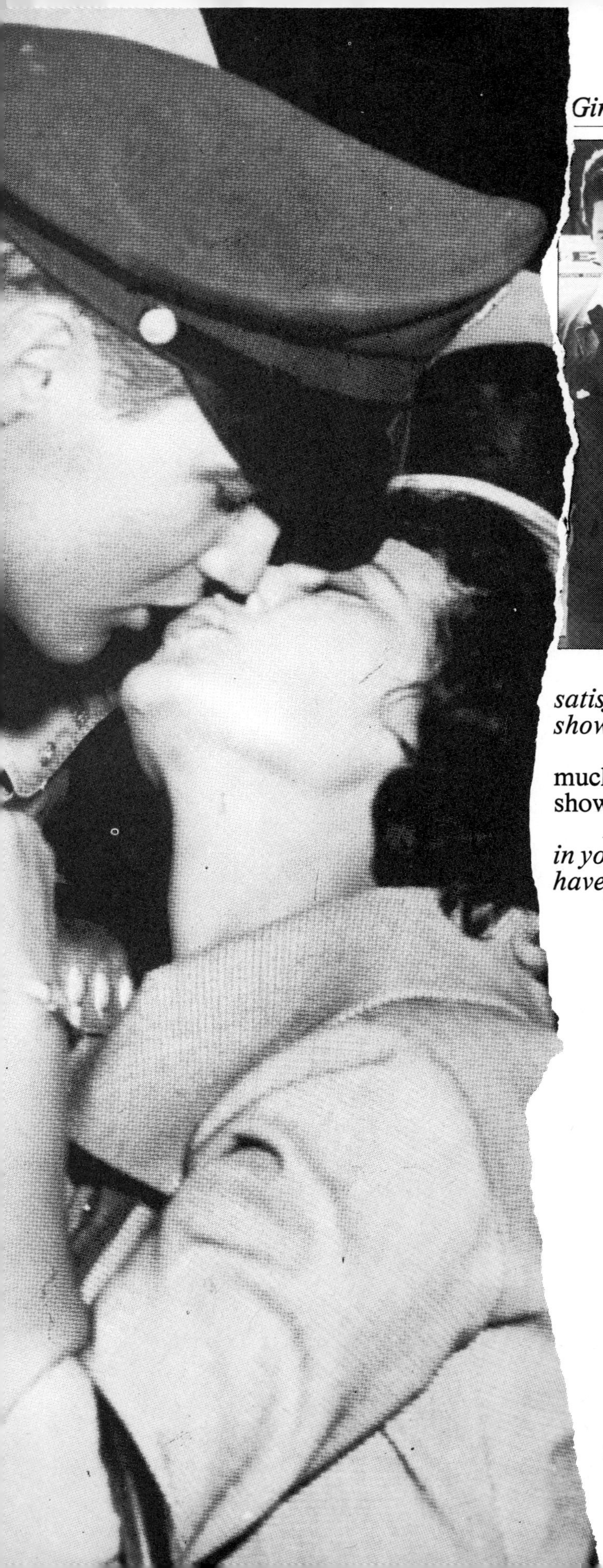

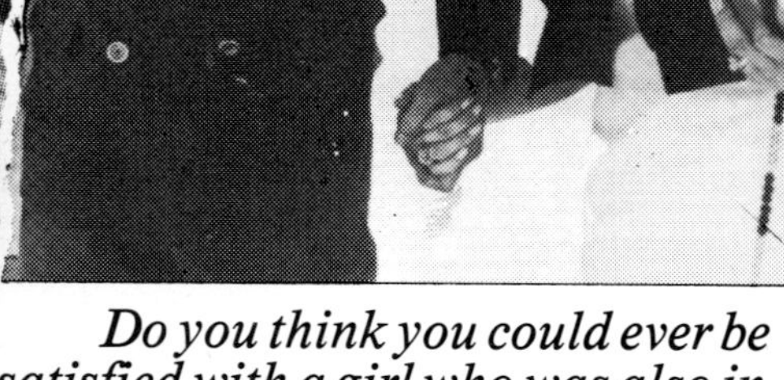

WITH PRISCILLA PRESLEY

Do you think you could ever be satisfied with a girl who was also in show business?

Actually, I don't think it'd make much difference whether she was in show business or driving a truck.

A lot of young people are interested in your views on marriage . . . Do you have an ideal age for guys to marry?

Well, as you're growing up, a lot of

MR. AND MRS. PRESLEY AND DAUGHTER LISA MARIE

times you think you're in love with somebody and you want to get married. A little later on in life you find out that you were wrong, that actually you didn't love them, you only thought you did. And I was no different. Several times I would probably have married, but my mother talked to me and said, you better wait and find out if this is

WITH JOAN BLACKMAN IN 'BLUE HAWAII'

what you want. And I did, and I was glad that I did.

When was the last time you thought you were in love?

Oh, many times, ma'am, I don't know. I suppose the closest that I ever came to getting married was just before

WITH JOCELYN LANE IN 'TICKLE ME', 1965

I started singing. In fact, my first record saved my neck.

When you get caught in a mob, have you ever been seriously hurt by girls?

I've been scratched and bitten and . . . (laughter).

What do you think about being scratched and bitten?

I just accept it with a broad mind because actually they don't intend to hurt you. It's not bad. They want pieces of you for souvenirs.

ELVIS AND HIS MOTHER

Elvis Faces The Fifties Press (Part One).

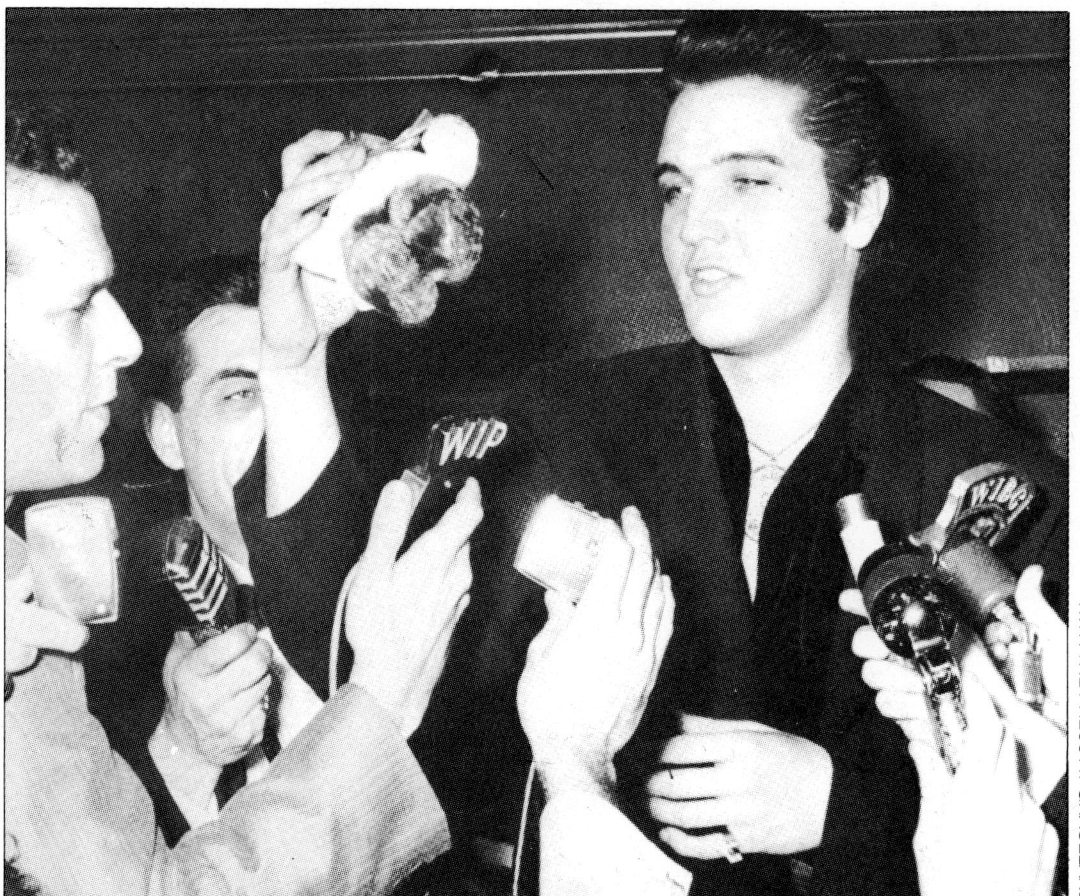

WITH THE PRESS AT GRACELAND

Are you happier now or were you happier when you were driving a truck and could have a quiet cup of coffee?

I'm happier now, in a lot of ways, and in some ways I was having a lot of fun then, you know.

Would you go overseas some day?

Yes, I would like to. I would like to.

Retirement? I'll never quit as long as I'm doing okay.

What do you consider doing okay?

Well, as long as there's a public, as long as you're pleasing the people, it'd be foolish to quit.

Elvis, would you like to say something to everybody out there tonight listening/etc/? Would you like to say hi to mom?

I sure would. I'd like to tell everybody how very much I appreciate it, how much I like them and everything,

THE FIRST GOLD RECORD

and I, I'll do my best to continue to please them and put out songs and movies.

How are you fixed for the future? What are your plans?

I have two music firms and then I have, like I said, a seven year contract with Paramount Pictures whereas each year I'm offered more money.

When you see things sold on the street, some saying 'I like Elvis' and others saying other things, do you get money each time? Do you get a percentage when they sell an 'I hate Elvis' button?

To be truthful, I really don't know. In fact I don't know who sells 'I hate Elvis' buttons.

One thing that's got to be a joke recently is the fact that when you join the army you'll have to have your hair cut. How do you feel about that? There'll be a lot of newspaper publicity about it. Does it bother you at all?

No, I don't care. It'll grow back. If

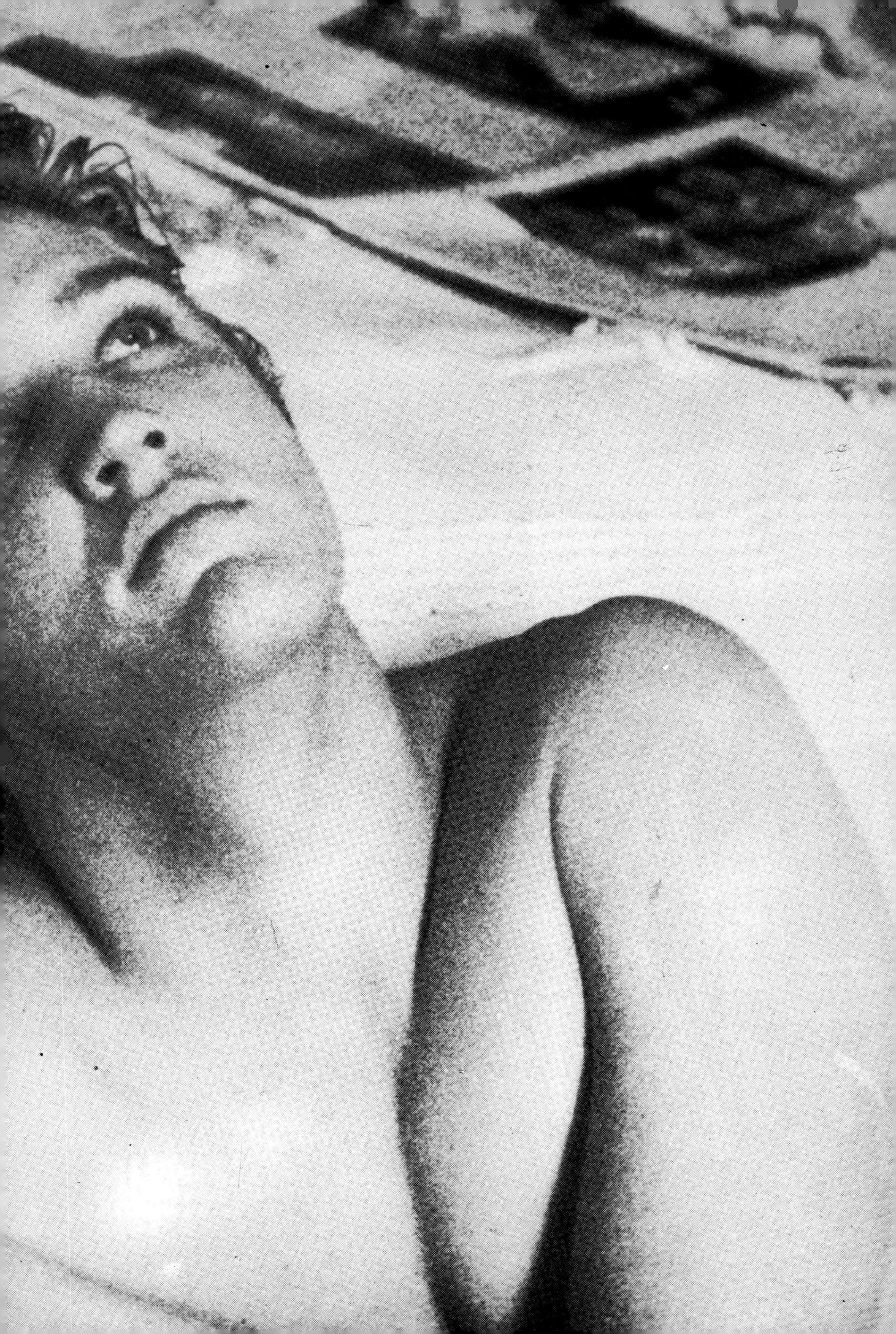

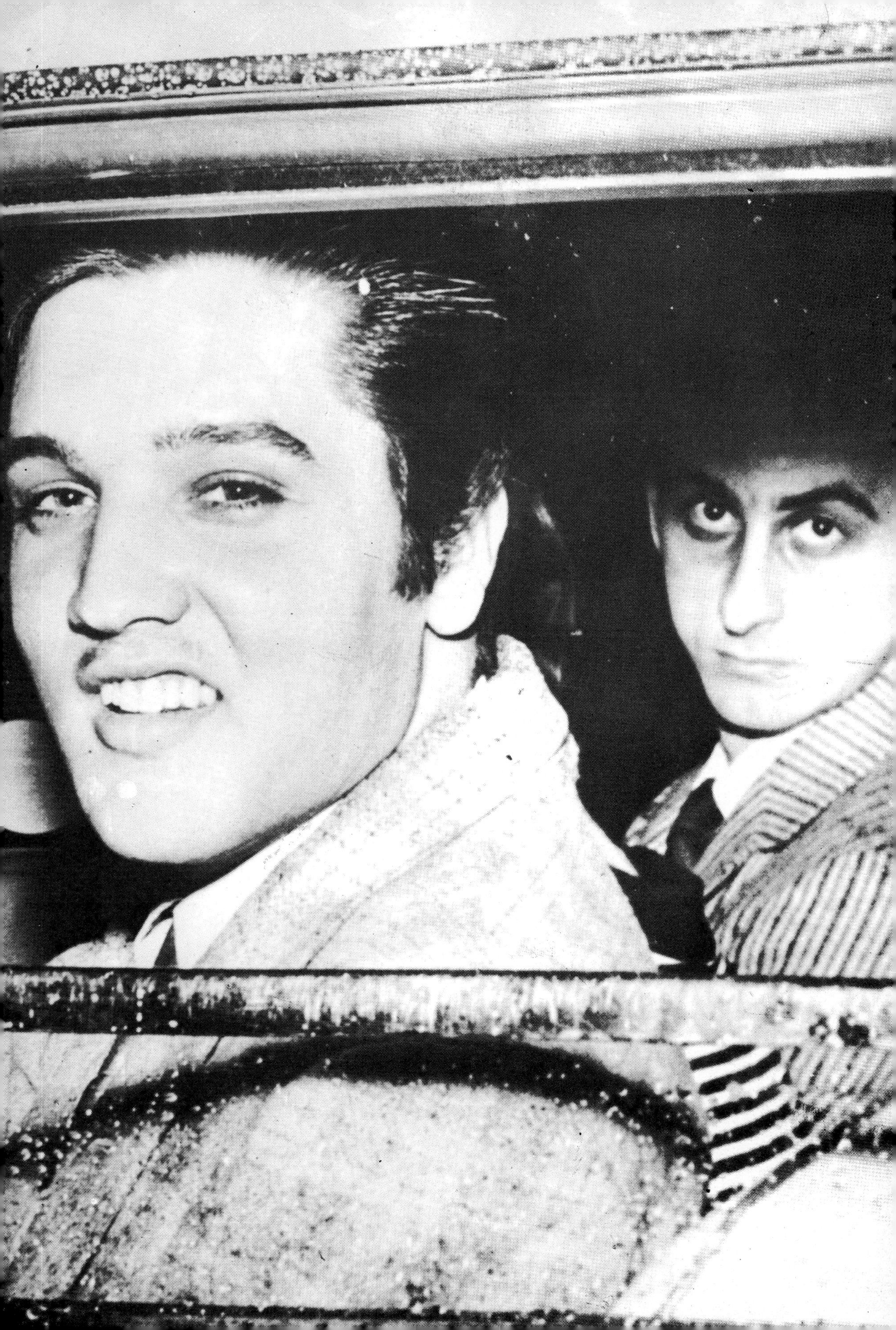

THE FIRST HARLEY-DAVIDSON

it was a case of cutting it off and never having any more, then I'd be worried.

What about the sideburns trademark?

Well, I'm stuck with them. I had them many years ago, when I was about sixteen years old. I just got stuck with them; I can't get rid of them now.

(There's a lady interviewer here whom I can't hear even on the record, but I think she asks something about friends and the 'entertainment world'.)

It has its advantages and its disadvantages.

Don't you seek privacy all the time?

Well, that's the main thing. I mean, naturally you don't go places like other people, you can't go to your local theatre and things like that. Like, back at home, whenever I want to see a movie, I have the theatre manager show it to me after the theatre closes up at night. They have a fairground there and I rent the fairground when it closes up, sometimes.

What's that beautiful ring on your left hand?

That's a star sapphire. A girl gave it to me in California. A lot of people can hurt you and not even realise they're doing it.

You don't have much of a private life now then, have you?

No sir, I haven't.

What about the rumour that you once shot your mother?

Well, I believe that one takes the

cake. That's the funniest one I ever heard.

How did it start?

I have no idea. I can't imagine. When you mentioned it to me it was the first time I ever heard it.

Do you smoke marijuana to help work yourself into a frenzy?

(Giggle, mumble.)

Do you find that touring is much more harder on you (sic) than making movies or TV?

Well, touring is the roughest part. It's really rough. You're in a town, you do a show, you come off, you ride in a car, you go on to the next town.

After a show, how do you like to taper down, after a big show like tonight?

Well, take for instance last night, we had a show in Vancouver and I didn't sleep till about ten o'clock today. I get all keyed up and it's hard to relax.

What do you do before the show to help you deal with some of the excitement, the tension?

I just walk around, slow . . .

I want to give you an opportunity here to go over a lot of the rumours that have been printed about you. Your style of gyrating while you sing has been widely criticised even by usually mild and gentle TV critics. Do you have any animosity towards them?

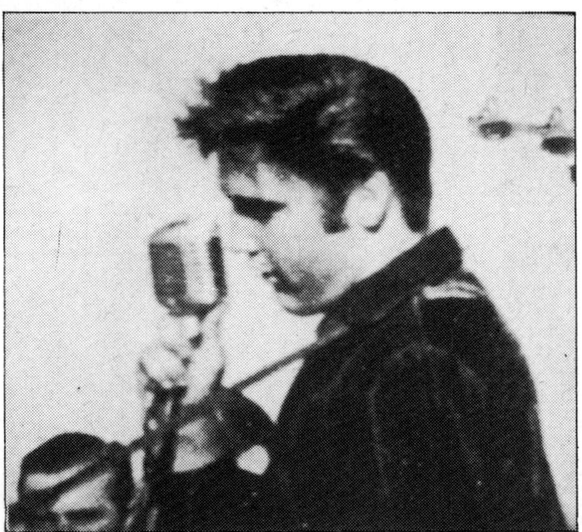

Well, not really. Most people have a job to do and they do it.

How do you find the reaction of young people toward you, mainly the girls? Do they know who you are and so forth?

Well (laughs), that's kind of a hard question.

That's real, real difficult because it's a leading question, Elvis, because I know of course, as I guess does everybody else, they go pretty crazy for you. Do you get along with them?

Yeah, I get along real well. Everybody, when I finish work and get home they come along . . . they bring their families, especially at weekends . . . and take pictures.

Must be a fairly exciting thing.

Yes it is, it's kind of exciting . . .

ON THE SET OF 'G.I. BLUES', 1960

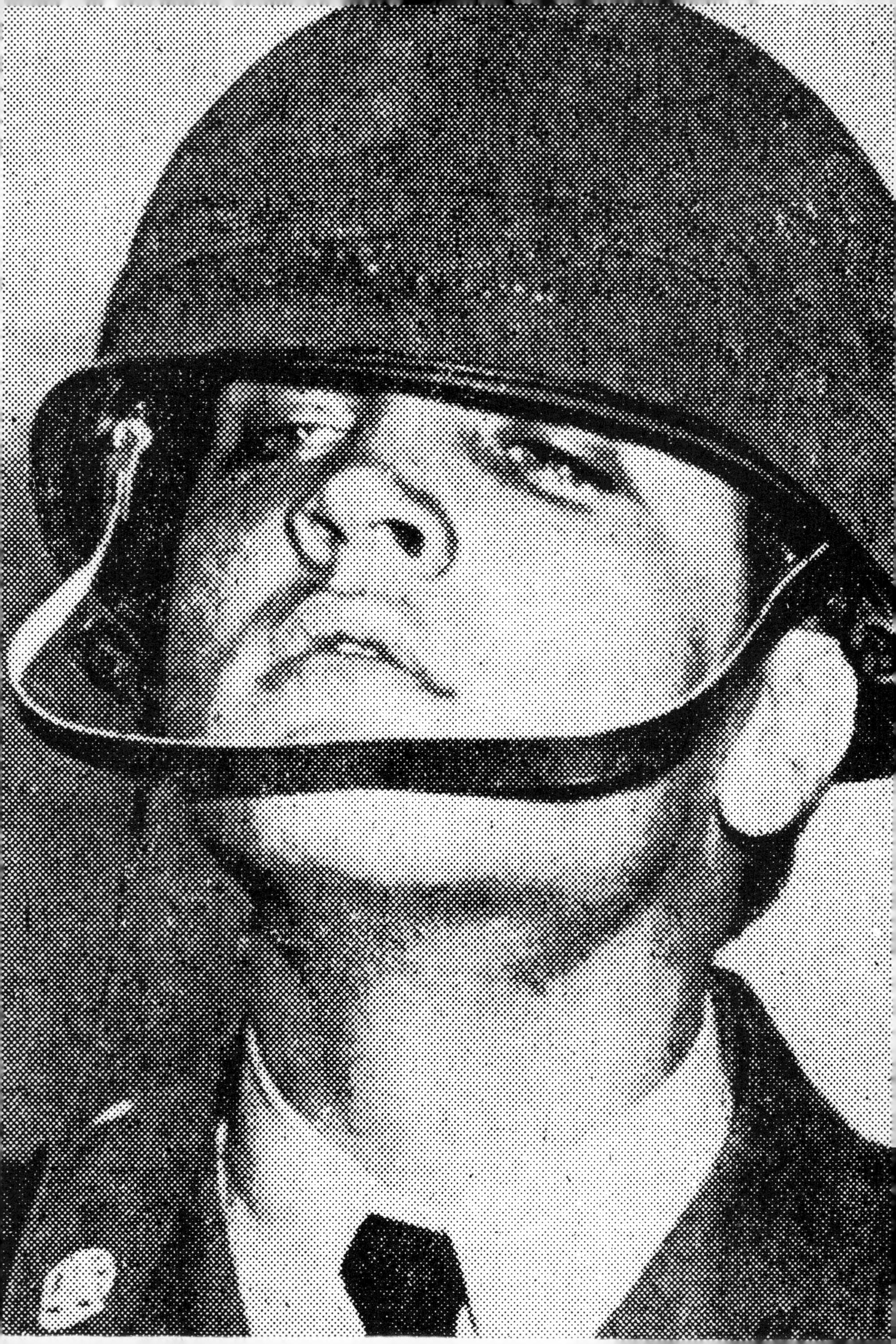

Elvis and Uncle Sam.

PRESLEY'S PARENTS VISIT HIM IN GERMANY

I learned a lot about people in the Army. I never lived with other people before and had a chance to find out how they think. It sure changed me, but I can't tell you offhand, how.

I never griped. If I didn't like something, nobody knew excepting me. If I'd been what they thought, I'd have got what was coming to me. But I never talked about show business. I went along.

As for the fans, they changed some, but they were still there.

When I got out of the Army, my first professional appearance was on a television show with Frank Sinatra. I was so nervous I wasn't sure I'd make it. Getting back to it wasn't as simple as I thought it'd be. But Frank was kind and understanding, and with his help and encouragement we taped the show okay.

Do you have a rougher time than most soldiers?

No, ma'am. Everything was straight down the middle. I've been treated no better nor any worse than any of the other boys, and that's the way I wanted it, because I have to live with the other boys, you know.

Not by the army, I mean by the other boys, do they treat you rough?

ELVIS INDUCTED INTO THE ARMY

Uncle Sam.

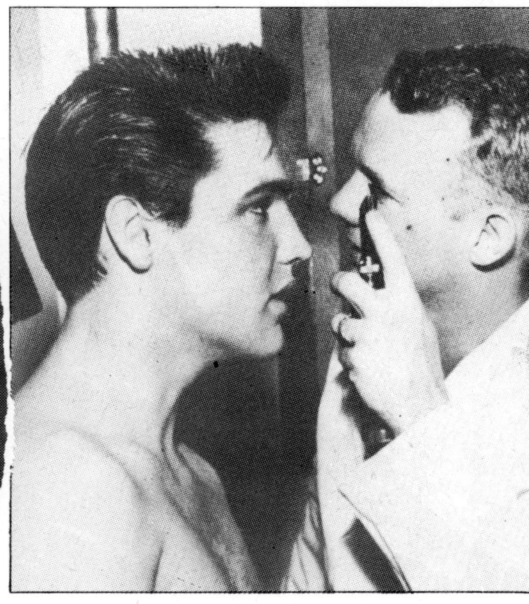

No, sir, not at all. I quite expected it because even when I'm a civilian I get harassed a little bit by a few people, you know, and I was expecting that, but when those guys looked around and they saw me pulling KP and marching with a pack on my back and everything, well, they figured, well, he's just like we are, so I get along very well with them and they're a good bunch of boys.

Have the other guys a nickname for you?

Quite a few.

SPEARHEAD

US

Elvis and Colonel Tom.

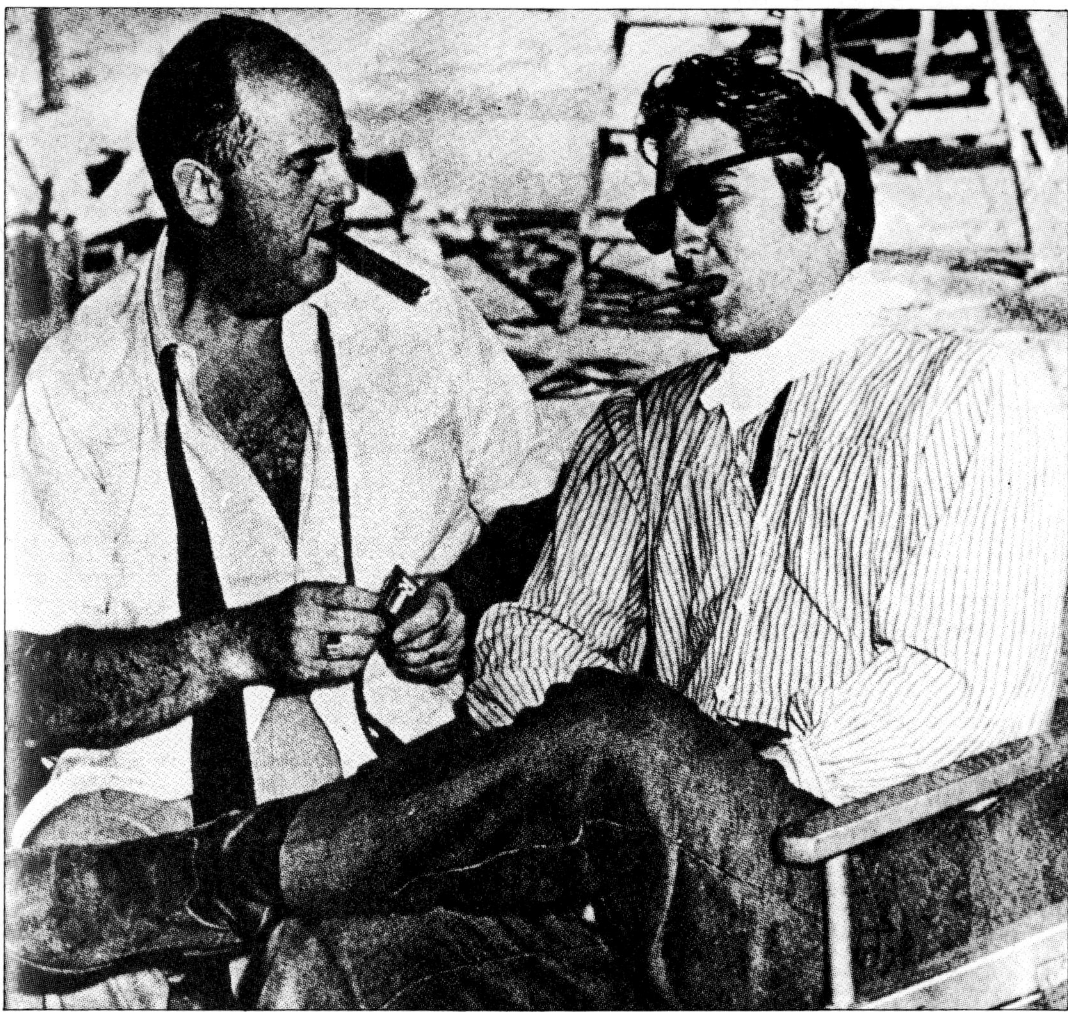

One morning I looked out of my bedroom window on the second floor facing the highway, and spotted a man picking up leaves outside the stone fence, and stuffing them in a valise.

I told my manager, Colonel Tom Parker, and he went out to check on things. He asked the man what he was doing with the leaves and the man said he'd got a big thing going up in Buffalo, New York, selling the leaves for souvenirs. He was selling them for 10 dollars a piece.

The Colonel admired the man's ingenuity so much, he let him go. The fella kept right on picking up leaves — just the choice ones — and putting them in his bag.

The Colonel got to thinking about the "leaf gimmick" as he called it, and contacted the local Memphis radio station. He invited them over to come

'THE TROUBLE WITH GIRLS', 1969

out and rake up 10 or 12,000 leaves and offer them as prizes in various Elvis Presley contests. My discs got a bigger than ever radio play and those leaves went like wildfire.

The Colonel is almost like a daddy to me when I'm away from home. He was like a boy with a new toy when I gave him a 26-foot plastic rowboat for his birthday. He immediately rushed it to the ocean and got her into the water. You should have seen him out there, grinning like a catfish, with that straw hat of his tipped back on his head.

What touched me was he christened the boat "Gladys" in honour of my Mama. That's the best present he could ever give me.

ELVIS

RCA
Victor

Elvis and Recording.

NEIL MATTHEWS, HOYT HAWKINS, ELVIS AND GORDON STOKER

For my recording sessions I work with ear musicians and not sheet musicians. They're great. You just hum, or whistle or sing a tune for them once and then they get to work, and inside a minute or two the joint is jumping.

I take my time to do the right thing. I can't properly explain it but it all begins with listening, and more listening. It all narrows down gradually. I listen for hours. For a week. Two weeks. When I'm down to the songs I think I'll want to do I call the session.

I can cut fifteen songs on a session. Me and the boys sometimes get together late at night and it's late morning when we call it a day.

As always, we released my "Blue Hawaii" and "Follow That Dream" albums right after the films were finished, and they stayed on the very top of the American hit parade for weeks, selling several hundred thousand.

I know right away which songs are right for me. When I'm picking songs for records, I listen to everything that comes in to my music company. It's screened first by someone who knows what I like. Some of them are first efforts like "Heartbreak Hotel" and "Don't Be Cruel". The author of the first one never wrote another. Any songs submitted to my hotel I handle directly. Folk songs and classics are

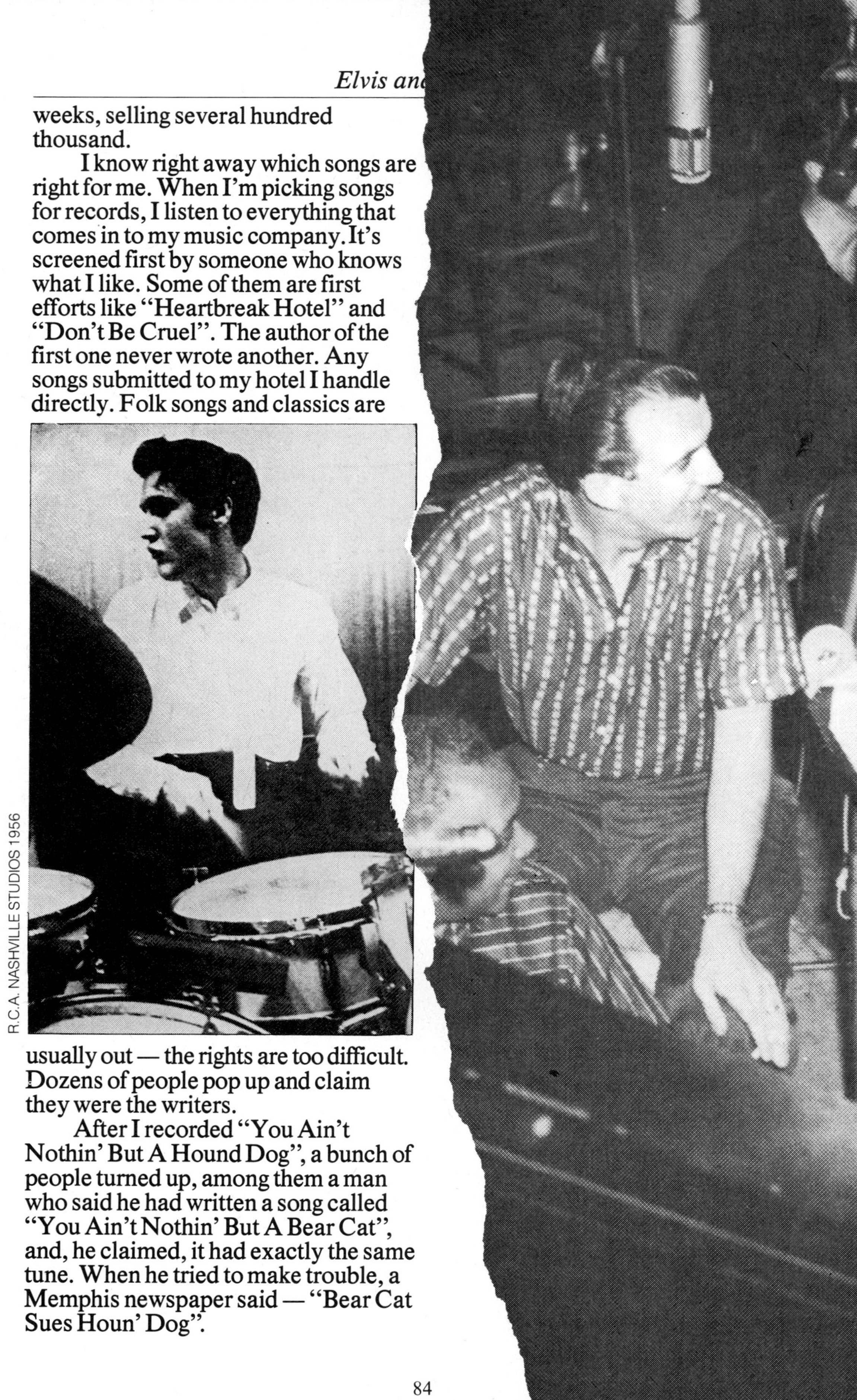

R.C.A. NASHVILLE STUDIOS 1956

usually out — the rights are too difficult. Dozens of people pop up and claim they were the writers.

After I recorded "You Ain't Nothin' But A Hound Dog", a bunch of people turned up, among them a man who said he had written a song called "You Ain't Nothin' But A Bear Cat", and, he claimed, it had exactly the same tune. When he tried to make trouble, a Memphis newspaper said — "Bear Cat Sues Houn' Dog".

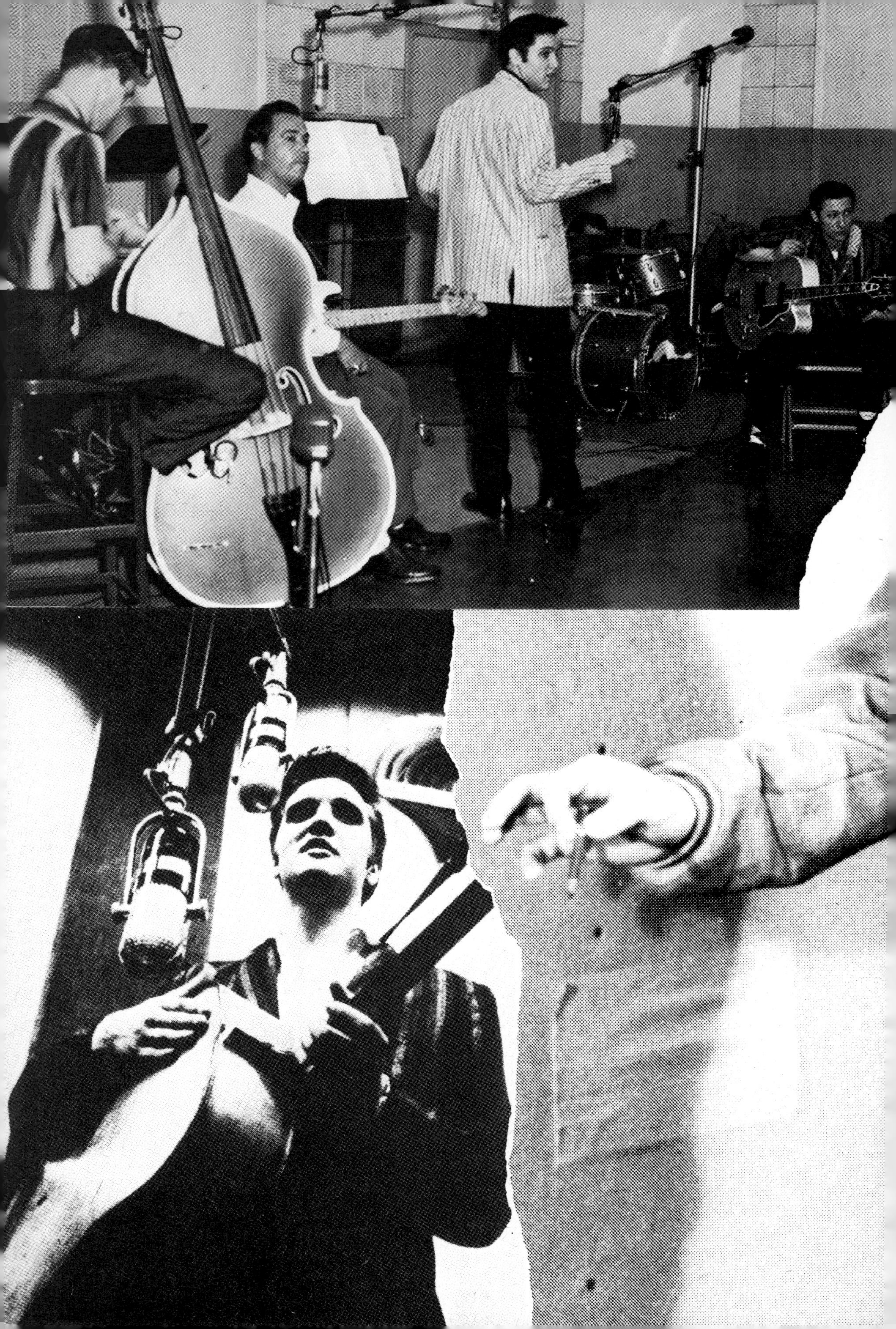

Elvis and The Critics.

ELVIS AND LIBERACE IN LAS VEGAS

I don't like to be called Elvis the Pelvis. I mean, it's one of the most childish expressions I ever heard, Elvis the Pelvis. But if they want to call me that there ain't nothing I can do about it so I have to accept it, like I accept the good with the bad, the bad with the good.

As a rule most of the adults are real nice. They're understanding. I've had them come up to me and say 'I don't personally like your kind of music but my children like it and if they like it I don't have to think about it but when I was young I liked the charleston, I liked the foxtrot, I liked this and that'. Adults are real intelligent. They don't run people into the ground for having a nice time.

I've tried to figure it out. I don't see how they can think that it would contribute to juvenile delinquency, someone only singing and dancing. I don't see that because if there's anything I've tried to do, I've tried to live a straight, clean life and not set any kind of a bad example.

You accept the bad along with the good. I've been getting some very good publicity, the press have been real wonderful to me, and I've had some bad publicity but you have to expect that, and I know I'm doing the best I can and I've never turned a reporter down, I've never turned a disc jockey down, because they're the people that helped make me in this business, and as long as I'm doing the best I can . . .

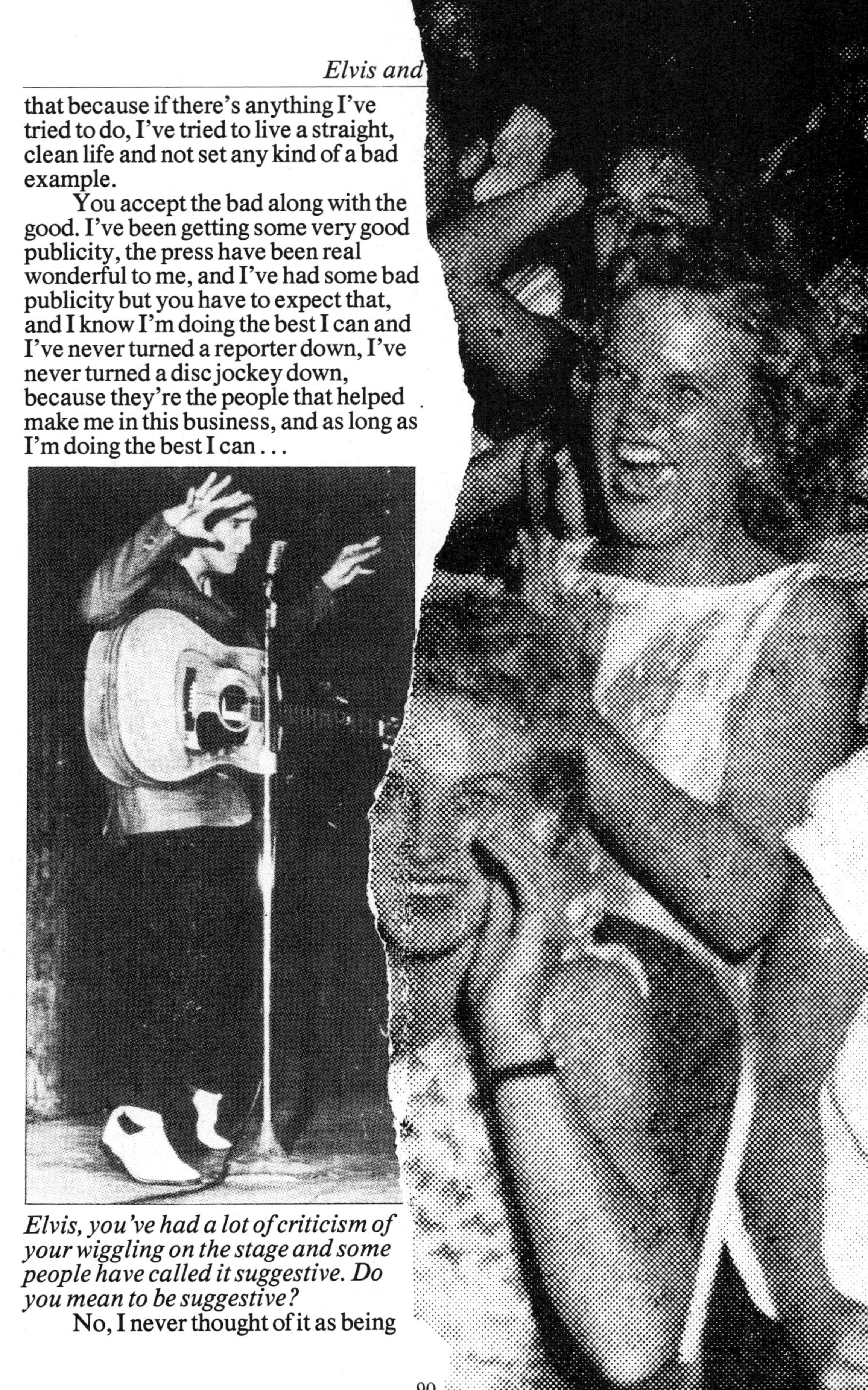

Elvis, you've had a lot of criticism of your wiggling on the stage and some people have called it suggestive. Do you mean to be suggestive?

No, I never thought of it as being

suggestive. That's just my way of expressing the songs.

You seem to be popular enough on your singing and appearance alone. Would you stop the wiggling if criticism grew too vast?

No sir, I can't.

Tone it down?

To be truthful, I can't do ballads nearly as well as I can do the other kind, because I don't have the voice for it.

Do you think disc jockeys made you?

Definitely, yes. If disc jockeys wouldn't play it the people wouldn't know of it so they wouldn't know what's happening, you know. I attribute it to a little bit of everything. I attribute it to the people who have accepted me, then the disc jockeys and the good handling I

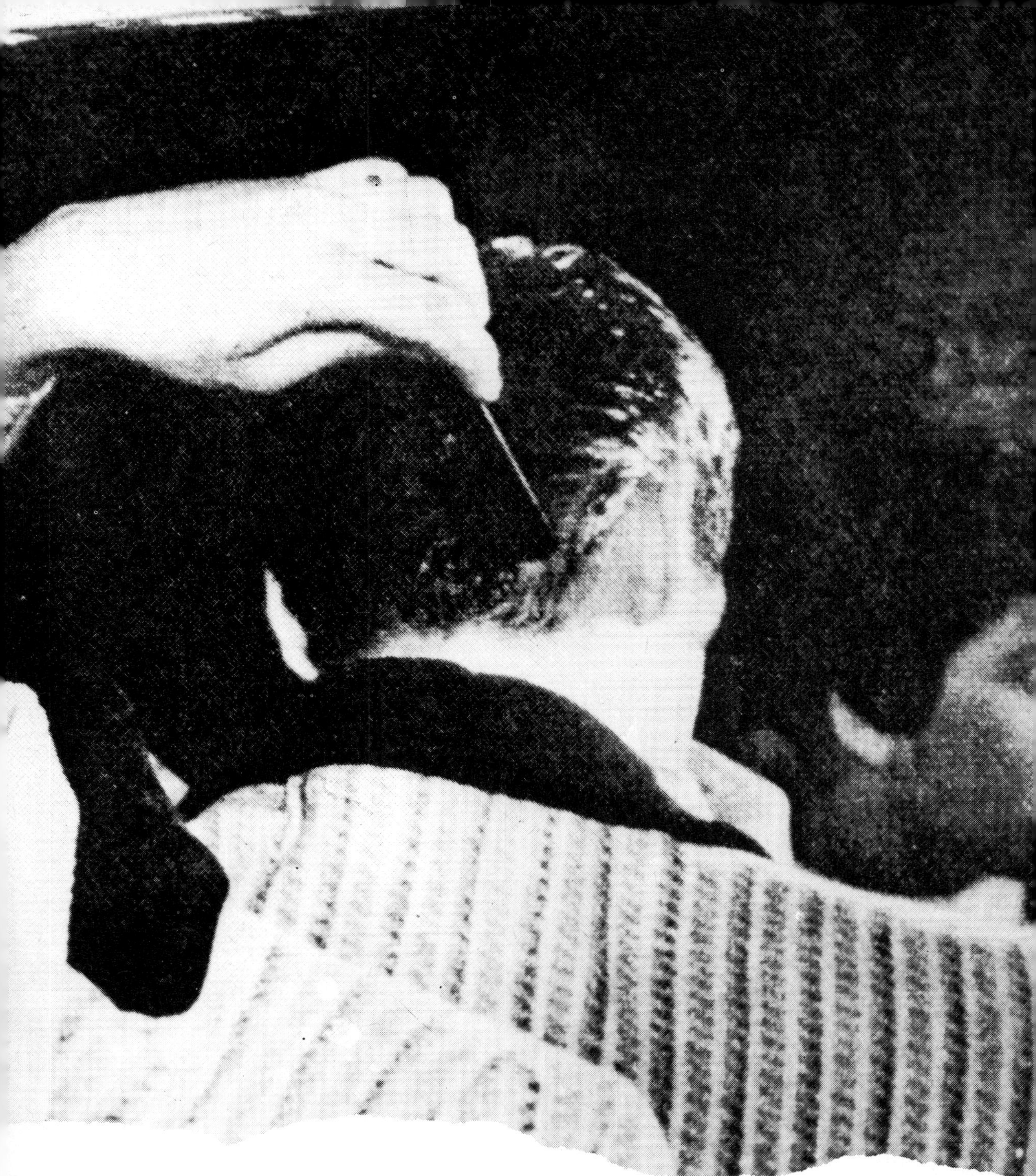

have had, the management and everything.

How do you feel about being asked questions about your personal life?. Do you think an entertainer should be asked questions about marriage and girls and . . .

Let's face the facts. Anybody in the public eye, their life is not as private any more. Everything you do, the public knows about it and that's how it's always been and that's how it'll always be. Critics never bother me, or change me neither. I don't have time to be bothered. I'm working too hard. And I'm figuring to stay around awhile.

Maybe some of the critics don't dig me. They've got a job to do, I guess. But I don't pay no attention. They're not touching me.

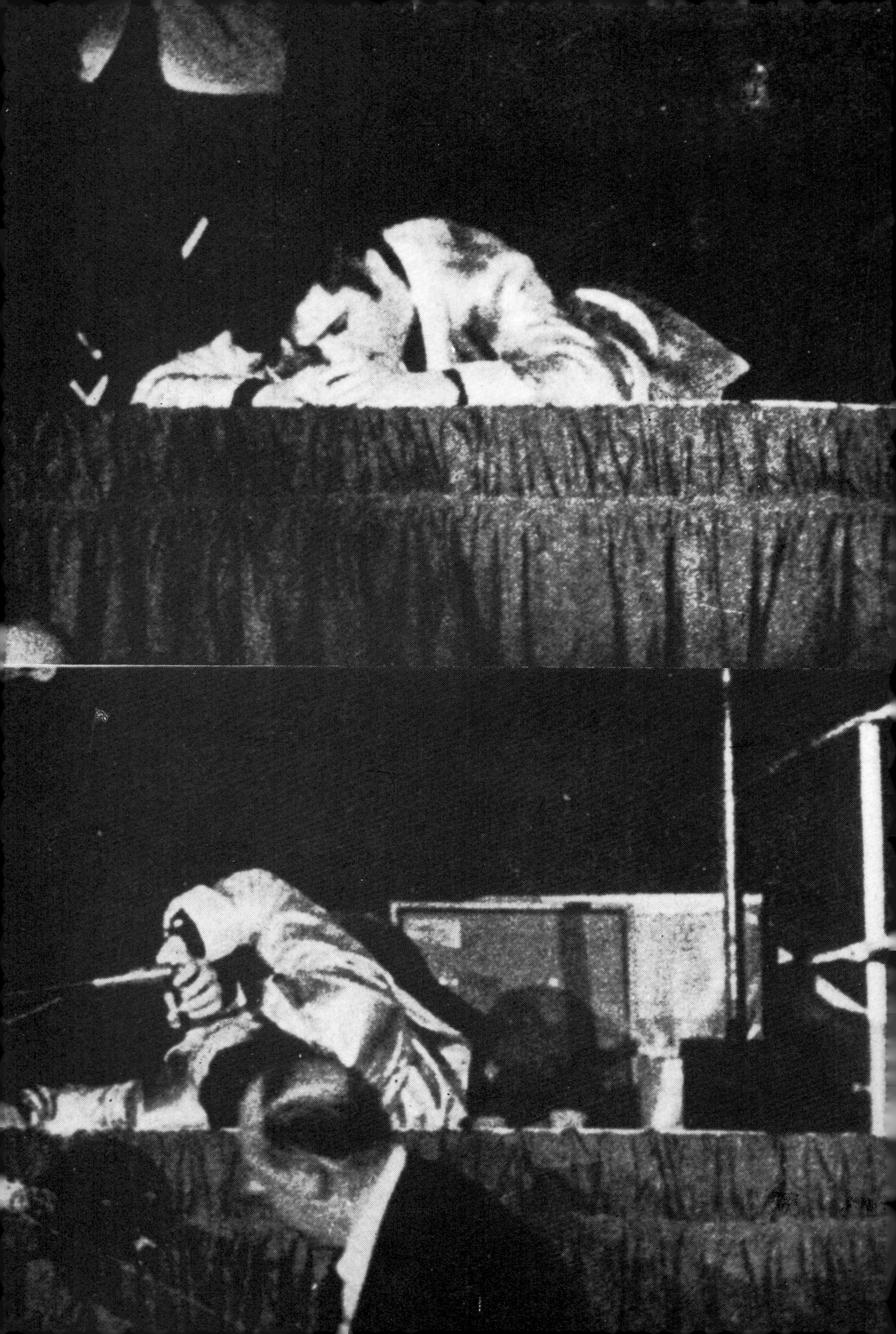

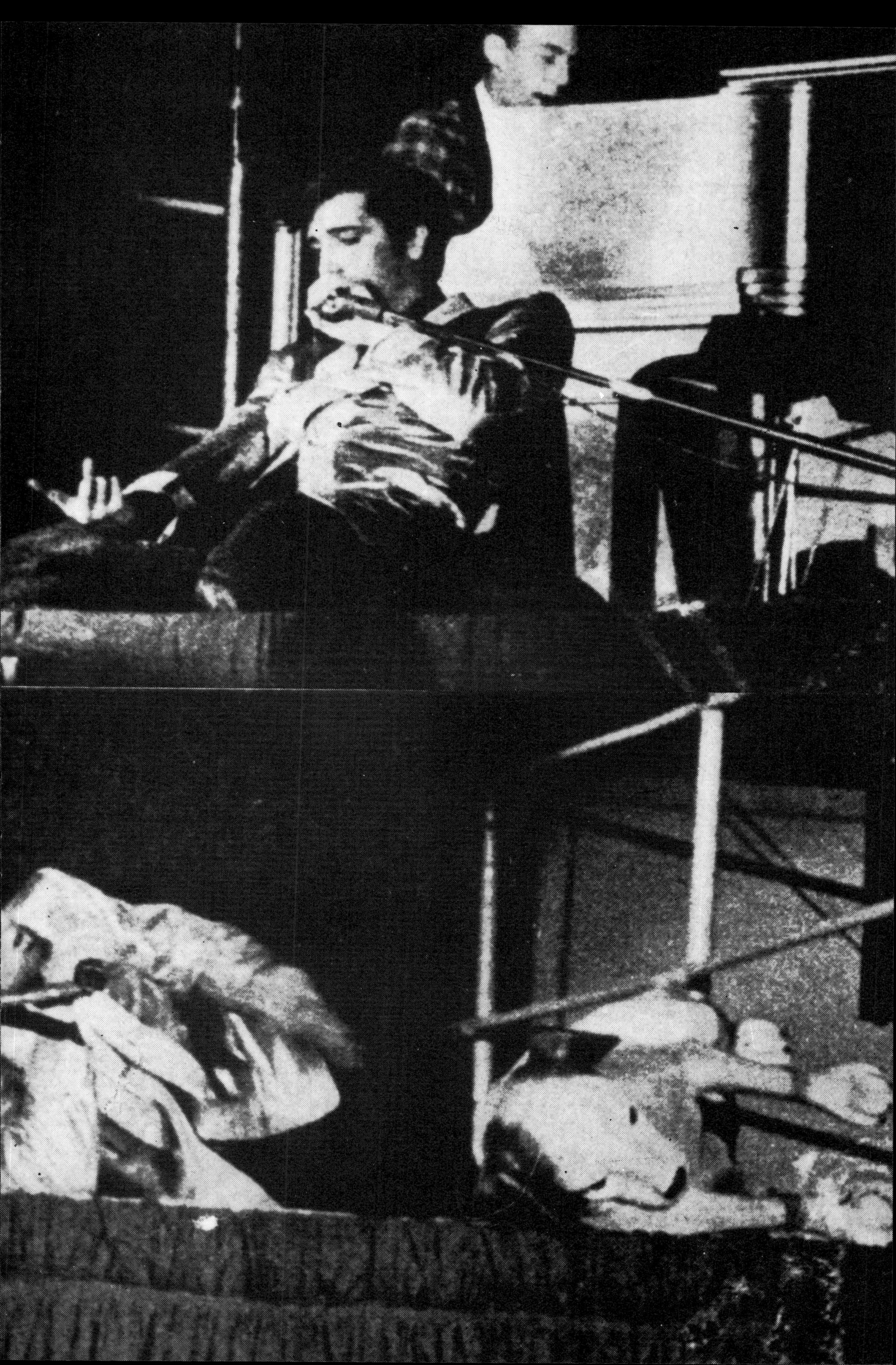

ULL 501

Elvis on Graceland.

WITH HIS NEW FRONT GATES, 1957

"Graceland" is just 15 miles south of Tupelo. When I first bought the estate and mansion for 100,000 dollars in 1958, it was just like living in the country. There was nothing around my place but a few cotton and sugar cane plantations. The highway was second class. Now the Tennessee highway department has resurfaced the highway that runs in front of my estate because the thousands of tourists constantly roaring past, parking, backing up, and turning around, had torn it up.

When the highway was put in top shape, it opened the way for a new flood of traffic and a big land boom. Now we're surrounded by all sorts of things I didn't plan on.

My fans don't embarrass me. They're the greatest. I love 'em. Even when they get a little rough, they're swell kids.

The mansion sits almost directly in the middle of its 14 acres, and things

GRACELAND, 3764 HIGHWAY 51, SOUTH MEMPHIS

are going crazy around the place.

A city block, a 25,000 square foot shopping centre, has gone up — one of those ultra-modern buildings. It has everything from clothes shops to supermarkets, barber shops, and even a record store in it. I'm right happy about the record shop.

But the point is it's all increasing the traffic in front of my place, until it's almost like living in New York's Times Square.

To the north, is a new, tall, white Baptist church. Across the highway, to the west, a real estate operator is advertising lots and modern homes at 17,500 dollars a piece. Tractors and bulldozers are ripping the land apart.

I got a lot of good decorating ideas for "Graceland". I'm always fixing and repairing around the house. I like to do things first class, too. I had one wall knocked out of the first floor of the house to enlarge the room. Then I got a wonderful idea to make the ceiling of my bedroom all velvet. I like bright

colours, like orange, red and yellow. They look right nice.

I'm real proud of my "Graceland". I'll never leave. If the invasion of my privacy keeps up, it can be easily remedied. We'll just have a solid string of weeping willow trees planted along the stone fence around the entire estate. That will at least keep the noise down and give us privacy.

I only really feel at home in Memphis, at my own "Graceland" mansion. It isn't that I don't like Hollywood. But a man gets lonesome for the things that are familiar to him; his friends and acquaintances. I know I do. That's why I would never live in Hollywood permanently.

Hollywood's a lovely city. I've learned to appreciate it more since we moved into a Mediterranean style villa I rent on a Bel-Air hilltop. It's so quiet up there. The place is all marble columns and statuary, a fine home from home. But home for me will always spell Memphis and "Graceland".

Elvis Faces The Fifties Press (Part Two).

Do you feel that rock and roll, the popularity of rock and roll will diminish in any way while you're in the army?

It's hard to tell. All I can say is I hope not.

Is it a relief to get away from all the autograph hunters and the hysterical females?

It is not. Once you get used to it, if nobody comes up and asks for an autograph or if no one bothers you, then you start worrying. As long as they come round, you know that they still like you and it makes you feel good.

I've read newspaper accounts about you where the other fellows seemed to get the end of your fist, what about these newspaper reports? Are they accurate?

Yes sir, I imagine.

Well, how come? Did you lose

your temper?

Just a case of get them or be got, you know.

What started the incidents most of the time?

Somebody hit me or tried to hit me. I mean, I can take ridicule or slander and I've been called names

THE FIRST SET OF PUBLICITY SHOTS, 1956

right in my face and everything, but I've had a few guys that've tried to take a swing at me and naturally I can't just stand there.

What's your favourite sport, Elvis?

Football.

You like playing football?

Yes.

Where were those pictures taken in a fan mag of you playing football?

They were taken in a park near my house.

Outside of Memphis?

Yes.

What about your famous collection of teddy bears? What started that?

Oh, that got started from a rumour. An article came out that I collect stuffed animals, and I was swamped with them. Actually I keep them because people give them to me, but I never even thought of collecting stuffed animals in my life.

Do you appreciate them now that you have them or do you just save them?

I keep them. I have them all over the walls and the chairs and everywhere.

IN PERSON
2 HOURS
MENT & FUN
Variety
Home
Convalescent
JULY 4TH 8 PM
RUSSWOOD
PAR

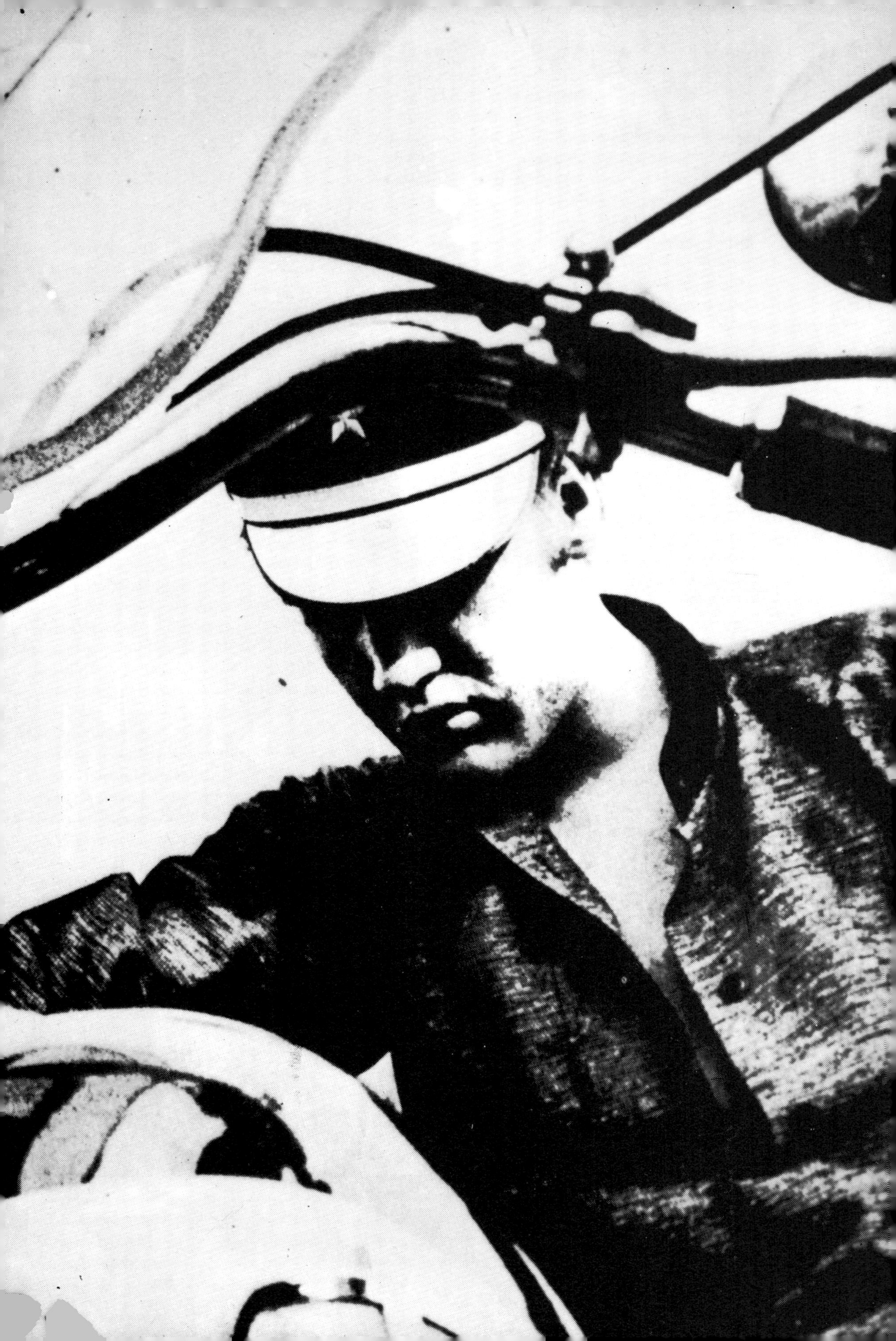

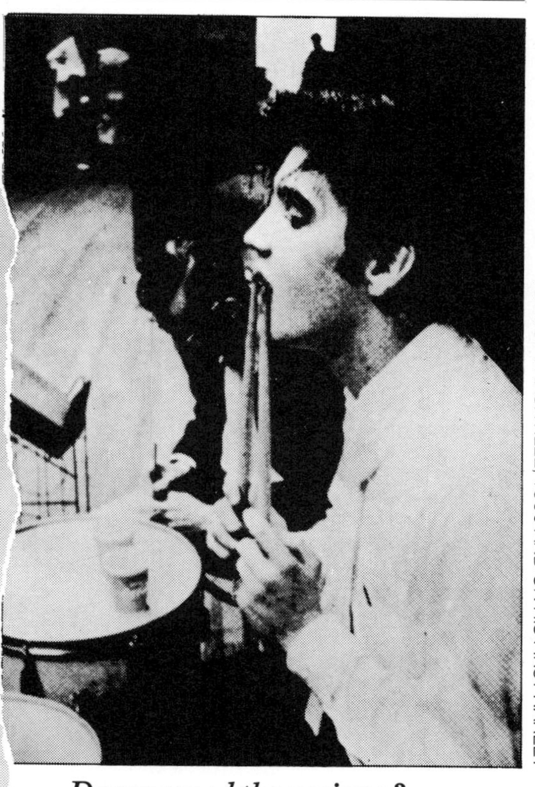

AT R.C.A. NASHVILLE, 1956 AND ON HIS FIRST HARLEY

Do you read the reviews?

Not if I can help it.

Do you keep a scrapbook at all?

Only of the good stuff.

What kind of a teenager were you? Would you consider yourself well behaved?

Yes. I was raised in a pretty decent home and everything. My folks always made me behave whether I wanted to or not.

How do they feel about your success and the things that some of the critics have said about you, both good and bad?

I guess they're just like myself. We always had a kind of a common life, we never had any luxuries but we were never real hungry, you know. And I guess they're just real proud, just like I am.

What do you do with four Cadillacs?

I don't know, I haven't got any use for four . . .

You gave one of them to your folks, is that right?

REVIVING A FAN

'JAILHOUSE ROCK'

Anything that's mine is theirs. I'm planning for seven, I mean, I want seven . . . I was thinking about a Presley used car lot.

I understand that you bought a home for your folks and even though your father is only 39 you insisted that he retire, is that true?

Yes, he's more help for me at home because he can take care of all my business and he can look after things while I'm gone.

You create a sort of mass hysteria amongst your audience of teenagers. When you shake and you quake when you sing, is that sort of an involuntary response to the hysteria of your audience?

Involuntary? I'm aware of everything I do at all times, but it's just the way I feel.

I mean for example if somebody's playing ball, they try just a little bit harder when their fans root, and I was wondering whether this had anything to do with it?

Oh sure. I guess any artist, when the audience looks like they're enjoying it, you put more into it.

Coming back to religious songs, if you should put an album out or an

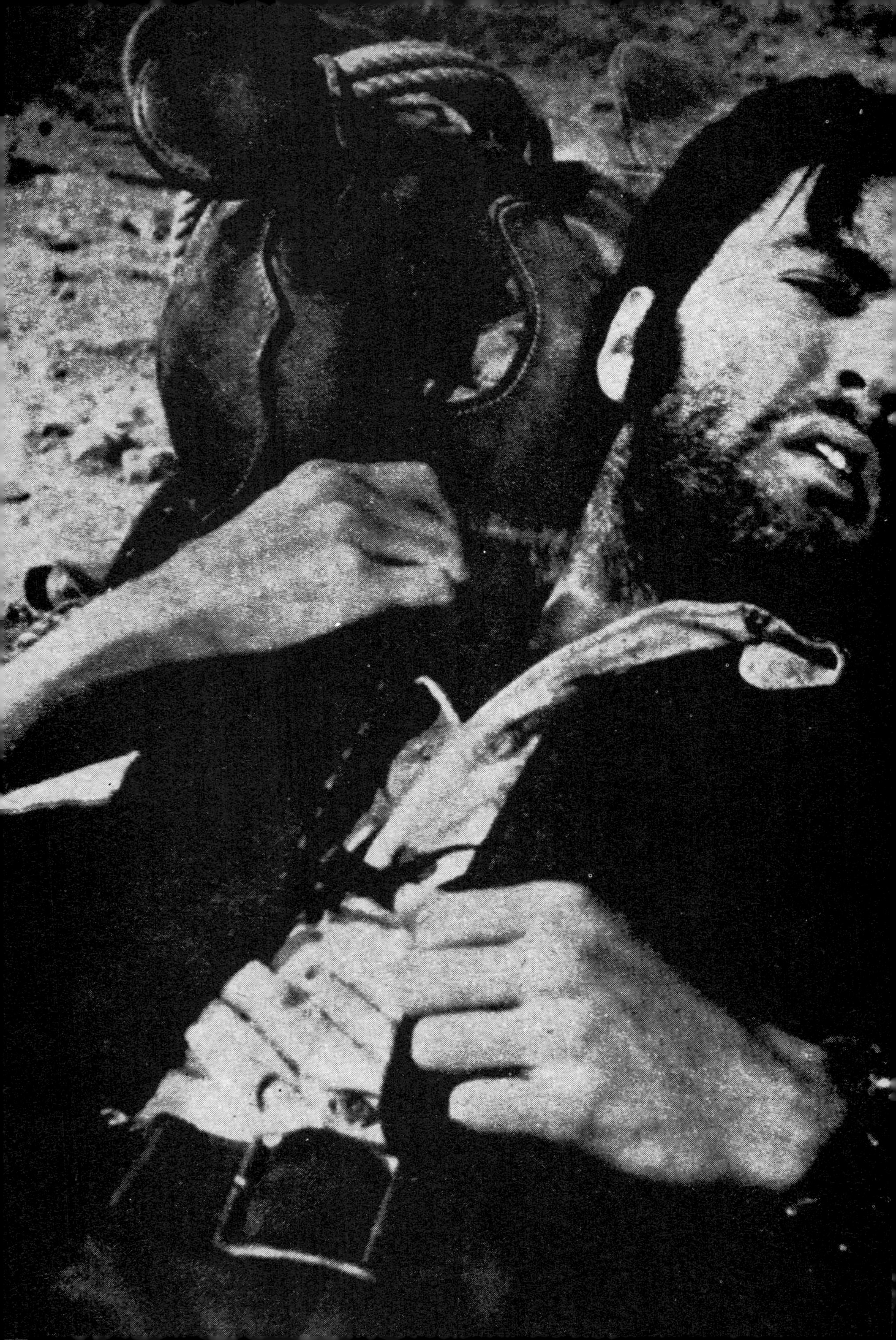

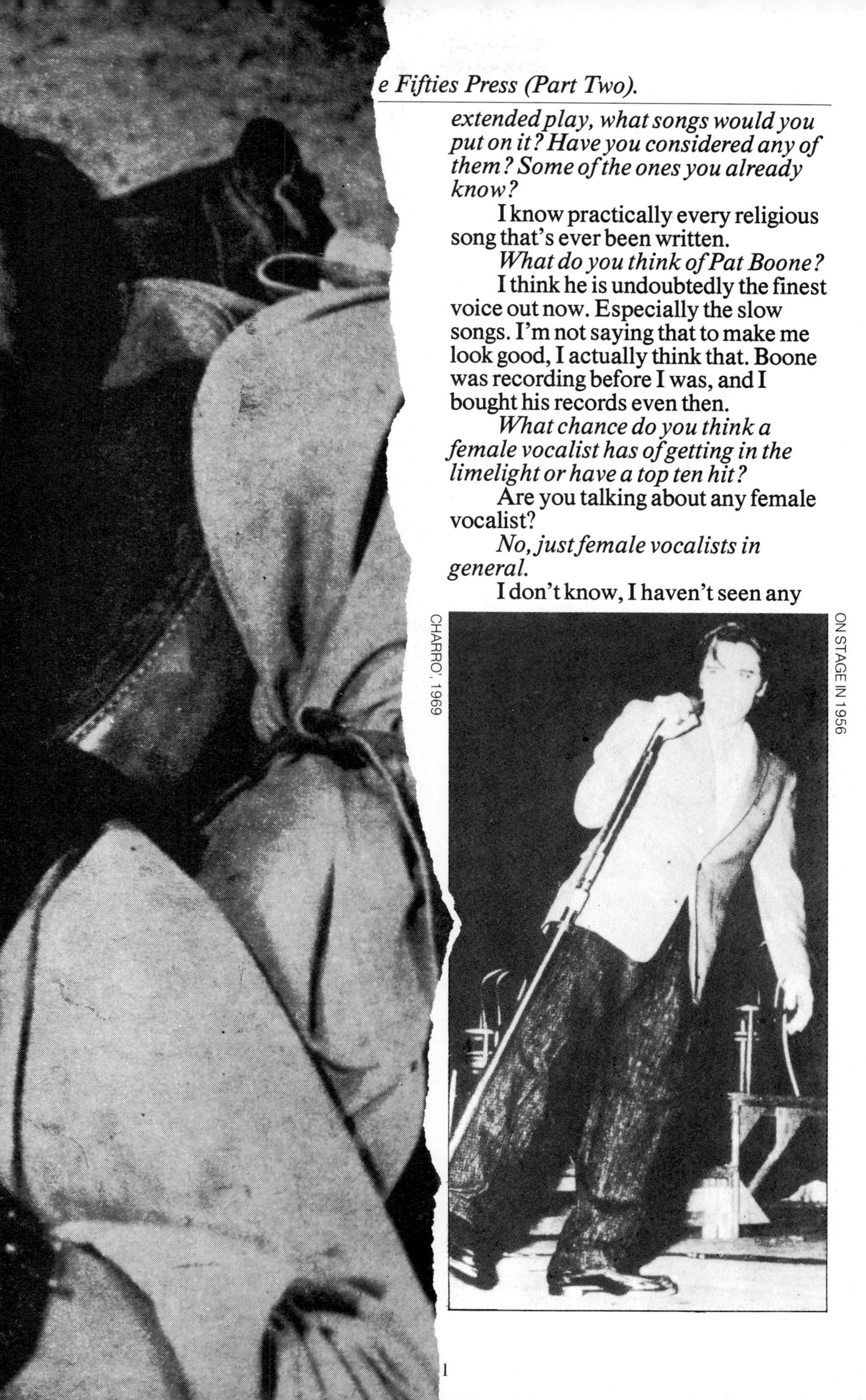

CHARRO', 1969

ON STAGE IN 1956

extended play, what songs would you put on it? Have you considered any of them? Some of the ones you already know?

I know practically every religious song that's ever been written.

What do you think of Pat Boone?

I think he is undoubtedly the finest voice out now. Especially the slow songs. I'm not saying that to make me look good, I actually think that. Boone was recording before I was, and I bought his records even then.

What chance do you think a female vocalist has of getting in the limelight or have a top ten hit?

Are you talking about any female vocalist?

No, just female vocalists in general.

I don't know, I haven't seen any

yet. I would imagine it's just according to the songs they sing. The material can make you or break you. If you sing a good song it's going to sell, if you sing a bad one it won't.

What is your favourite female singer right now?

Patti Page and Kay Star.

What is your favourite song that you've recorded?

"Don't Be Cruel".

It's been said that your only extravagances have been your cars. Is that accurate?

Yes, it's accurate. I just never realised how extravagant it was because . . .

R.C.A. NASHVILLE, 1956

I have too many, I mean, nobody drives them, they just stand there and the tyres go down. Actually I don't need four, I just went crazy.

What about your shirts?

I'll tell you what I did the other day. I had a German made Messerschmidt, a little car, and there's a guy there in town that's been wanting that Messerschmidt for the last year. He owns a clothing store, one of the top clothing stores in Memphis, so I went up there today and I told him, I said, you've been wanting this car so bad, I

ELVIS AND SCOTTY MOORE

said, I want a deal with you. I said, you let me pick out all the clothes I want. So I was there for about two hours and a half and the store was a wreck when I left.

What do you think about serious music? Do you ever listen to it?

Serious music?

Like opera, symphony.

Truthfully, I don't understand it. I'm not going to knock it, I just don't understand it. Just like I don't understand jazz.

Anything else particular you

ELVIS AND THE JORDANAIRES

want to tell us?

Well, I'd like to tell you that I sure appreciate all the help you've been giving me and I'd like to tell you how much I appreciate all the wonderful people that have been writing in and buying my records and coming out to see the shows, because after all that's what makes anybody is the people, they make you or break you.

I want to entertain people. That's my whole life — to my last breath. More than anything, I want to be a good actor. The kind that is around for a long time. But I don't want to ever stop singing.

When music starts I gotta move.

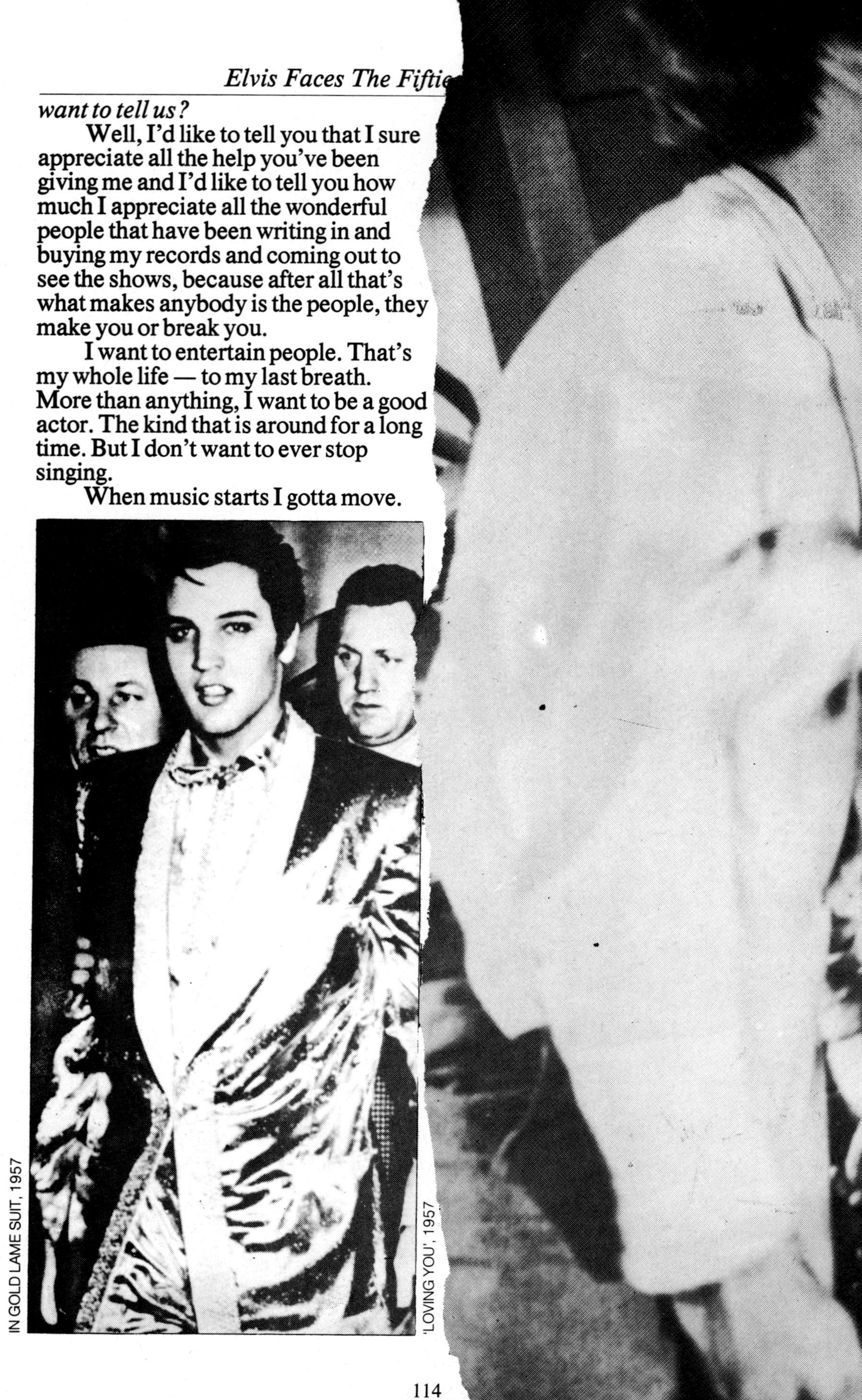

IN GOLD LAME SUIT, 1957

'LOVING YOU', 1957

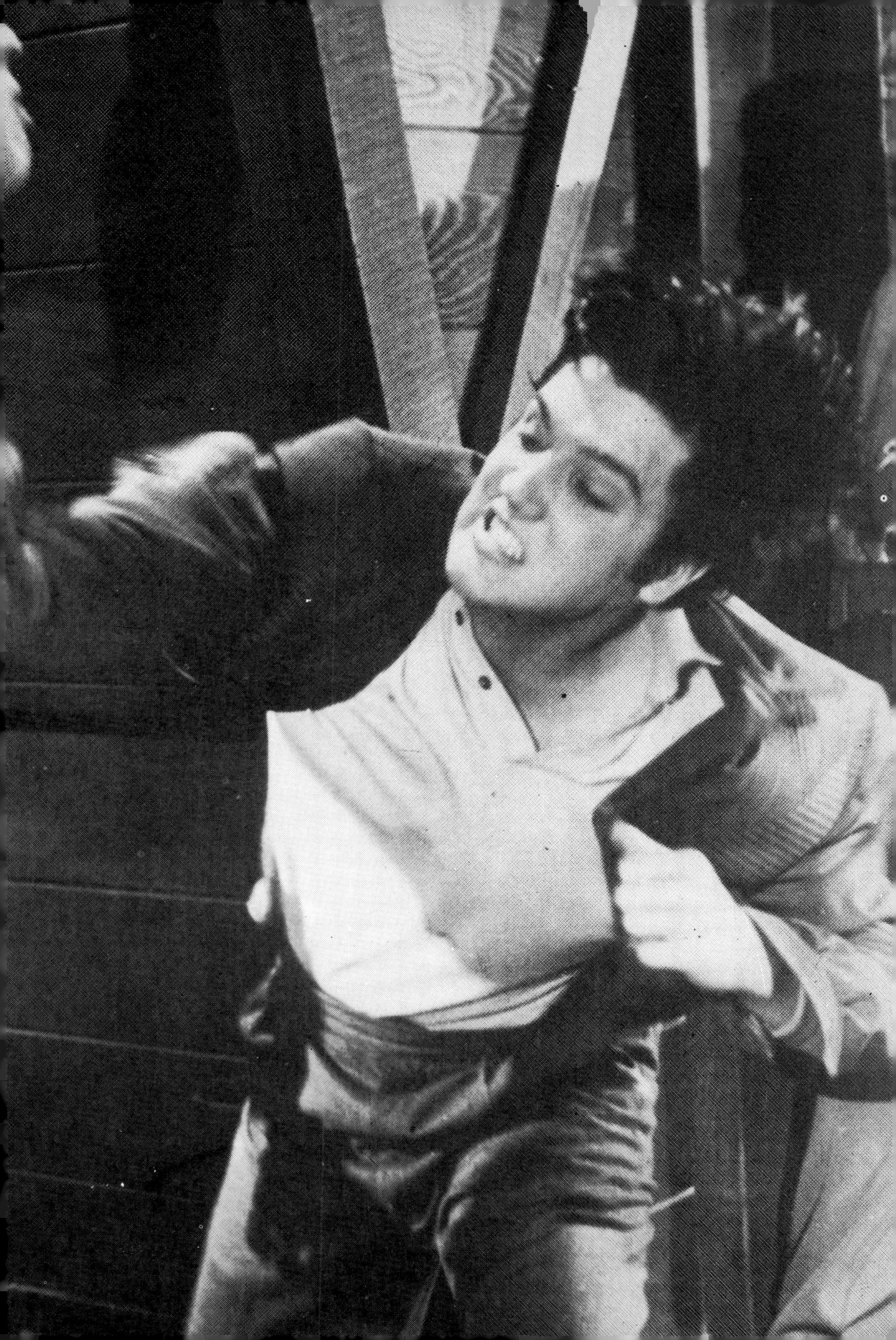

AGED TWENTY-TWO IN 'JAILHOUSE ROCK' AND FORTY-TWO AT ONE OF HIS LAST STAGE APPEARANCES

The Last Statement To The Press.

I'd like to tell you a little about how I got into this business and how I got started, where and when and so forth, because it's been written up so many times that people don't really know the true story. It happened when I was just out of high school and I was driving a truck. I was studying to be an electrician and I got wired the wrong way somewhere along the line.

I went into a recording studio and I made a record for a guy named Sam Phillips. Sun Records. And he puts the record out in about a week. I went on driving a truck and just forgot about it. And when it came out they started play-

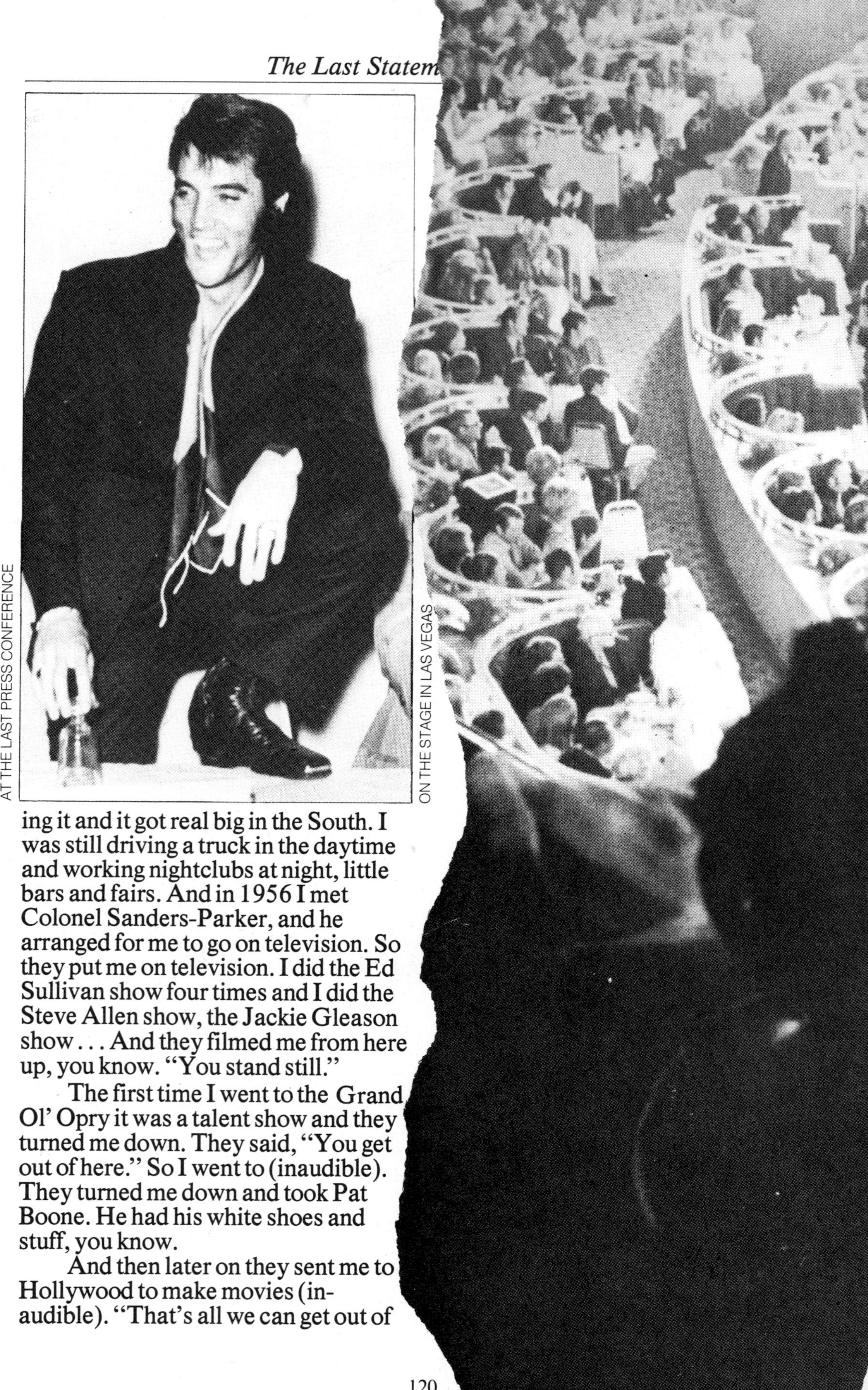

AT THE LAST PRESS CONFERENCE

ON THE STAGE IN LAS VEGAS

ing it and it got real big in the South. I was still driving a truck in the daytime and working nightclubs at night, little bars and fairs. And in 1956 I met Colonel Sanders-Parker, and he arranged for me to go on television. So they put me on television. I did the Ed Sullivan show four times and I did the Steve Allen show, the Jackie Gleason show . . . And they filmed me from here up, you know. "You stand still."

The first time I went to the Grand Ol' Opry it was a talent show and they turned me down. They said, "You get out of here." So I went to (inaudible). They turned me down and took Pat Boone. He had his white shoes and stuff, you know.

And then later on they sent me to Hollywood to make movies (inaudible). "That's all we can get out of

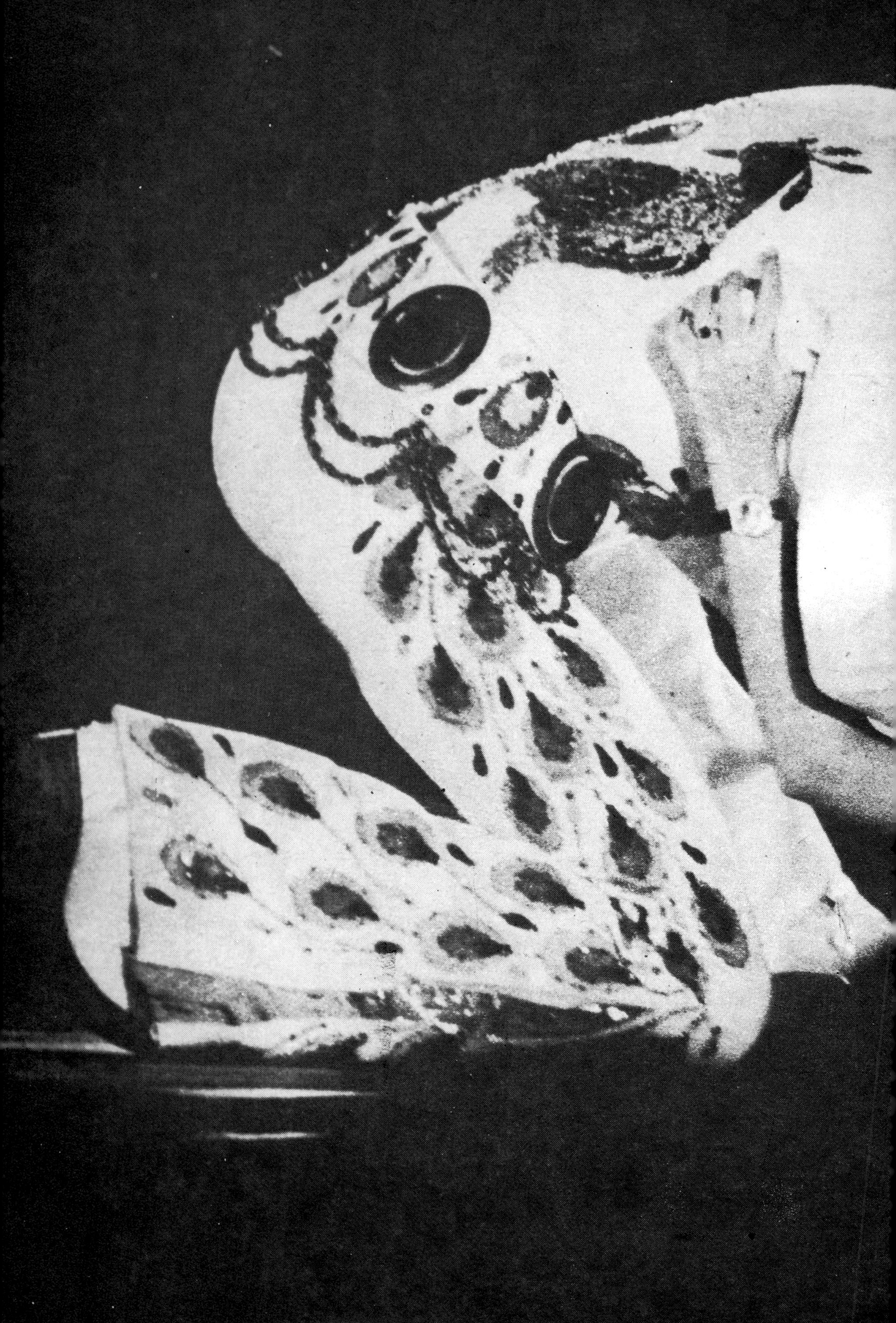

THE INTERNATIONAL HOTEL LAS VEGAS

him." So I made four movies. In 1958 I got drafted. I went into the army and I stayed a couple of years and it was loads of fun. They made a big deal out of it and cut my hair. Then I came out and I made a picture called "G.I. Blues" where I thought I was still in the army. I made more movies, "Blue Hawaii"... It kind of got into a routine and a rut and I kind of wanted to come back and work live in front of people again.

I hope I haven't bored you.

THE FUNERAL PROCESSION MOVES DOWN ELVIS PRESLEY BOULEVARDE MEMPHIS, 1977

Pearce Marchbank is a product of Central School of Art, London, and Architectural Design, Rolling Stone, Friends, Oz, Time Out, and the music industry. He is at present editor and art director for a music publisher and for Omnibus Press, and has a number of his own books in print.

Mick Farren is a product of St. Martin's School of Art, London, and the '60's underground press. He has, at one time or another, sung with various rock 'n' roll bands. Four of his science fiction novels are currently in print, and he contributes regularly to *New Musical Express* and other publications.